# UNIPART

## MOTORISTS ATLAS
## GREAT BRITAIN
## & NORTHERN IRELAND

THIS IS YOUR UNIQUE REGISTRATION NUMBER. USE IT TO ENTER THE FREE COMPETITION. JUST FILL IN THE REGISTRATION FORM ON PAGE 135. YOU CAN GO A LONG WAY WITH THE UNIPART ATLAS

## TENERIFE COMPETITION

**RULES OF ENTRY**

1. The Unipart Atlas Competition is open to the general public.
2. It is not open to employees of the Unipart Group of Companies, its Wholesalers,advertising and promotion agents or their families.
3. There are no cash alternatives to the prizes.
4. The closing date for entries is December 31st 1991.
5. The judges decision is final.
6. No purchase is required.
7. All winners will be notified by post.

8. No responsibility can be accepted for non-delivery or lateness of entries.
9. Winners who are under the age of 18 on their holiday departure date, must be accompanied by a parent or guardian.
10. The holiday is to be taken in the early part of 1992.
11. Entries wil be declared void if illegible, mutilated or incomplete in any way.
12. Free entry forms can be obtained by writing to Unipart House, Cowley, Oxford OX4 2PG

# Does this Atlas Really Contain Over £45 Worth of Vouchers?

We believe you will find your Atlas invaluable in use, containing so much more than just an 'ordinary' atlas.

You'll see from the Contents Page (Page iii) just what we mean but please accept with our compliments over £45.00 worth of discount vouchers. The money-off vouchers in this Atlas can be used against a host of high quality Unipart DIY and Accessory products, they provide a real saving in these cost conscious days ! See page ix for details.

So, if it's a high quality clutch for an Alfa or an oil filter for a Zastava, with Unipart The Answer is YES...... Now what's the Question?

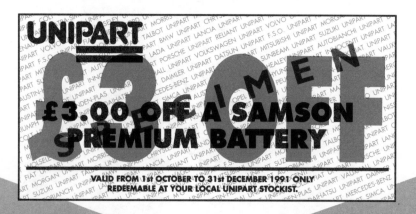

## The Answer is YES. Now what's the Question?

Bartholomew
A Division of HarperCollins Publishers
Duncan Street
Edinburgh
EH9 1TA

© Bartholomew 1991
© Unipart Group Limited 1991

Printed in England by R R Donnelley Ltd. (Ben Johnson Division), York & London.

ISBN 0 7028 1715 5

# Contents

# HOLIDAY BLACKSPOTS

To help you avoid those traditional holiday traffic jams AA Roadwatch have put together a list of the places to avoid. Delays build up at all these places most weekends from June through to September, the times to avoid these routes are 2 p.m. – 8 p.m. Fridays and 9 a.m. – 1 p.m. Saturdays. On occasional weekends traffic does not clear until 11 p.m. on Fridays, to hear the latest traffic conditions just call one of the numbers below.

**TO SOUTH COAST RESORTS**

**HAMPSHIRE/DORSET**

| | | |
|---|---|---|
| 1. A33 | Winchester bypass between M3 and M27. Added problems until late 1991 due to construction work. | |
| 2. A35 | Around Poole and Bournemouth. | |
| 3. A30 | Shaftesbury at junction with A350. | |
| 4. A351/A352 | Through Wareham to Swanage, Corfe Castle and Weymouth. | |

**KENT/SUSSEX**

| | |
|---|---|
| 5. A299 | Through Whitstable, Herne Bay and onto Ramsgate. |
| 6. M2 | At end of motorway (junction 7). |
| 7. A20 | Between Hollingbourne and Ashford and between Folkestone and Dover. |
| 8. A23 | North of Brighton and through Croydon and Purley. |

**SOUTH WALES**

| | |
|---|---|
| 9. M4 | Severn Bridge delays at toll booths and across bridge. Junctions 42 to 44 North of Swansea where traffic goes onto A48. |
| 10. A477 | Into Tenby and Pembroke. |

**NORTH WALES**

| | |
|---|---|
| 11. A55 | Delays to North Wales resorts along non dual carriageway sections. |

**WEST COUNTRY**

**DEVON**

| | |
|---|---|
| 12. M5 | Delays at the junctions near Exeter (J29, J30, J31). |
| 13. A38 | Around Plymouth. |
| 14. A380 | Into Torbay (Brixham, Paignton & Torquay). |

**AVON**

| | |
|---|---|
| 15. M32 | Avoid travelling into Bristol from M4 between 8 and 9 a.m. weekdays. |

**MIDLANDS**

| | |
|---|---|
| 16. M5/M6 | Interchange very busy most evenings 5 p.m. – 8 p.m. in all directions. |

**NORTH**

| | |
|---|---|
| 17. M6 | Junction 32 (M55 to Blackpool) traffic can back up from Blackpool along M55. |
| 18. A19 | Feeder route to North East resorts between Middlesbrough and Newcastle. |

**SCOTLAND**

| | |
|---|---|
| 19. A74 | Liable to delays between the border North of Carlisle and Abington (start of M74). |
| 20. A90/M8/M9 | Approaching Forth Road Bridge. |

**NORTHERN IRELAND**

There are no predictable holiday traffic jams in this region.

### Phone before you go

| | |
|---|---|
| National Motorways | 0836 401 110 |
| M25 London Orbital | 0836 401 127 |
| West Country | 0836 401 111 |
| Wales | 0836 401 112 |
| Midlands | 0836 401 113 |
| East Anglia | 0836 401 114 |
| North West England | 0836 401 115 |
| North East England | 0836 401 116 |
| Scotland | 0836 401 117 |
| Northern Ireland | 0836 401 118 |

Calls charged at 34p per minute cheap rate, 45p per minute at all other times.

**KEY**

⊤ BBC Local Radio

⌒ Holiday Blackspots

# WEATHER CENTRES

**For personal advice call the Meteorological Office**

| | |
|---|---|
| Aberdeen | 0224 210574 |
| Birmingham | 021-782 4747 |
| Bristol | 0272 279298 |
| Cardiff | 0222 397020 |
| Glasgow | 041-248 3451 |
| Kirkwall | 0856 3802 |
| Leeds | 0532 451990 |
| London | 071-836 4311 |
| Manchester | 061-477 1060 |
| Newcastle | 091-232 6453 |
| Norwich | 0603 660779 |
| Nottingham | 0602 384092 |
| Plymouth | 0752 402534 |
| Southampton | 0703 228844 |
| Sullom Voe | 0806 242069 |
| Northern Ireland | 08494 22339 |

# WEATHER HAZARDS

A comprehensive guide to weather hazards including: ferry crossings that are liable to cancellation, roads that are affected by high winds, and other seasonal information can be found on page xvi.

# WEATHER FORECAS

| | |
|---|---|
| National | 0898 5004 |
| **Regions:** | |
| Greater London | 0898 5004 |
| Kent, Surrey and Sussex | 0898 5004 |
| Dorset, Hampshire & I. O. W. | 0898 5004 |
| Devon and Cornwall | 0898 5004 |
| Wilts, Gloucs, Avon and Somerset | 0898 5004 |
| Berks, Bucks and Oxon | 0898 5004 |
| Beds, Herts and Essex | 0898 5004 |
| Norfolk, Suffolk and Cambridge | 0898 5004 |
| West, Mid and South Glam and Gwent | 0898 5004 |
| Salop, Herefs and Worcs | 0898 5004 |
| Central Midlands | 0898 5004 |
| East Midlands | 0898 5004 |
| Lincs and Humberside | 0898 5004 |
| Dyfed and Powys | 0898 5004 |
| Gwynedd and Clwyd | 0898 5004 |
| NW England | 0898 5004 |
| W and S Yorkshire and Yorkshire Dales | 0898 5004 |
| NE England | 0898 5004 |
| Cumbria and Lake District | 0898 5004 |
| SW Scotland | 0898 5004 |
| W Central Scotland | 0898 5004 |
| Edinburgh, S Fife, Lothian and Borders | 0898 5004 |
| E Central Scotland | 0898 5004 |
| Grampian and E Highlands | 0898 5004 |
| NW Scotland | 0898 5004 |
| Caithness, Orkney, Shetland | 0898 5004 |
| Northern Ireland | 0898 5004 |

# RADIO INFORMATION

This atlas has been designed to help smooth your way to easier motoring and make it as trouble-free as possible. However, accidents and roadworks can cause unpredictable delays so we recommend that you tune in to the local radio station wherever you happen to be travelling for up to the minute information. You should be prepared to make detours en route to reach your destination with the minimum of delay and you will find this atlas of great assistance in doing so. Many local radio stations operate an 'eye-in-the-sky' helicopter service to update local traffic information, especially during rush hour. One such service is the Unipart Flying Fox, operating in Oxford: just one small example of how Unipart sets out to serve the Motorist.

## NATIONAL RADIO INFORMATION

BBC National Radio gives frequent road weather information. Frequencies used are:–

|  |  | kHz/meters | V.H.F.(MHz) |
|---|---|---|---|
| Radio 1 | M.W. | 1053/285 |  |
|  |  | 1089/275 |  |
| (Bournemouth) |  | 1485/202 |  |
| (Merseyside) |  | 1107/271 |  |
| (available in some areas) |  |  | 98.2 - 98.8 |
| (National Coverage Due in 1992) |  |  |  |
| Radio 2 | M.W. | 693/433 | 88 - 90.2 |
|  |  | 909/330 | 88 - 90.2 |
| (Cardigan Bay) |  | 990/303 | 88 - 90.2 |
| Radio 4 | L.W. | 198/1515 | 92.4 - 94.6 |
| (Llangenplwyt) |  | 198/1515 | 104.0 |
| (Aberdeen) | M.W. | 1449/207 | 92.4 - 94.6 |
| (Carlisle) |  | 1485/202 | 92.4 - 94.6 |
| (London) |  | 720/417 | 92.4 - 94.6 |
| (Plymouth) |  | 774/388 | 92.4 - 94.6 |
| (Redruth) |  | 756/397 | 92.4 - 94.6 |
| (Tyneside) |  | 603/498 | 92.4 - 94.6 |
| (Scotland) |  | 810/370 | 92.4 - 94.7 |
| (W Scotland) |  | 810/370 | 97.6 - 99.8 |
| (Radio Solway) |  | 585/513 |  |
| (Radio Aberdeen) |  | 990/303 |  |
| (Radio Wales) |  | 882/340 |  |
| (Radio Clwyd) |  | 657/457 |  |
| (Mid Wales) |  | 1125/267 |  |
| (Radio Gwent) |  |  | 95.1 - 95.9 |
| (Radio Cymru) |  |  | 92.4 - 94.6 |
| (South Wales) |  |  | 96.8 |
| (Radio Ulster) |  |  | 92.4 |

## BBC LOCAL RADIO

Local radio stations giving road and weather reports

| M.W.kHz/meters | V.H.F.(MHz) |  |
|---|---|---|
| Radio Bedford | 630/476 | 95.5 |
| (North Beds) | 1161/258 | 103.8 |
| Radio Bristol | 1548/194 - 1323/227 | 95.5 |
| (Bath) |  | 104.6 |
| (Bristol) |  | 94.9 |
| (Somerset Sound) | 1323/227 |  |
| Radio Cambridgeshire | 1026/292 | 96.0 |
| (Peterborough) | 1449/207 | 95.7 |
| Radio Cleveland | 1548/194 | 95.0 |
| (Whitby) | 1548/194 | 95.8 |
| Radio Cornwall (Mid & West) | 630/476 | 103.9 |
| (North & East) | 657/457 | 95.2 |
| (Isles of Scilly) |  | 96.0 |
| Radio Cumbria (North) | 756/397 | 95.6 |
| (West) | 1458/206 |  |
| Radio Derby | 1116/269 | 94.2 |
| (Sutton Coldfield) | 1116/269 | 104.5 |
| (Stanton Moor) | 1116/269 | 95.3 |
| Radio Devon (North) | 801/376 | 103.4 |
| (Exeter) | 990/303 | 95.8 |
| (Plymouth) | 855/351 | 103.4 |
| (Torbay) | 1458/206 | 103.4 |
| (Okehampton) |  | 96.0 |
| Radio Essex | 765/392 | 103.5 |
| (South East) | 1530/196 | 95.3 |
| (North East) | 729/412 | 103.5 |
| Radio Furness (South Cumbria) | 837/358 | 96.1 |
| (Kendall) |  | 95.2 |
| (Windermere) |  | 104.2 |
| Radio Gloucestershire | 603/498 | 104.7 |
| (Stroud & area) |  | 95.0 |
| Radio Hereford & Worcester |  |  |
| (Hereford) | 819/366 | 94.7 |
| (Worcester) | 738/406 | 104.0 |
| Radio Humberside | 1458/202 | 95.9 |
| Radio Kent |  | 96.7 - 104.2 |
| (Hoo) | 1035/290 |  |
| (Littlebourne) | 774/388 |  |
| (Rusthall) | 1602/187 |  |
| 15 Radio Lancashire | 855/351 - 1557/193 |  |
| (Central & West) |  | 103.9 |
| (East) |  | 95.5 |
| (North) |  | 104.5 |
| 16 Radio Leeds (Farnley) | 774/388 | 92.4 |
| (Wharfedale) | 774/338 | 95.3 |
| 17 Radio Leicester | 837/358 | 95.1 |
| 18 Radio Lincolnshire | 1368/219 | 94.9 |
| 19 Radio London | 1458/206 | 94.9 |
| 20 Radio Manchester | 1458/206 | 95.1 |
| 21 Radio Merseyside | 1485/206 | 95.8 |
| 22 Radio Newcastle (Charlton) | 1458/206 | 96.0 |
| (Pontop Pike) | 1458/206 | 95.4 |
| (Fernham) | 1458/206 | 104.4 |
| 23 Radio Norfolk (East) | 855/351 | 95.1 |
| (West) | 873/344 | 104.4 |
| 24 Radio Northampton | 1107/271 | 104.2 |
| (Geddington) | 1107/271 | 103.6 |
| 25 Radio Nottingham | 1521/197 | 103.8 |
|  | 1584/189 | 95.5 |
| 26 Radio Oxford | 1485/202 | 95.2 |
| 27 Radio Sheffield | 1035/290 | 88.6 |
| (Holme Moss) | 1035/290 | 104.1 |
| 28 Radio Shropshire | 756/397 | 96.0 |
| (Ludlow) | 1584/189 | 95.0 |
| 29 Radio Solent | 999/300 | 96.1 |
| (Bournemouth) | 1359/221 | 96.1 |
| 30 Radio Stoke-on-Trent | 1503/200 | 94.6 |
| 31 Radio Sussex (Central & South) | 1485/202 | 95.3 |
| (Crawley & North) | 1368/219 | 104.5 |
| (East) | 1368/219 | 104.0 |
| 32 Radio Wiltshire Sound (North) | 1368/219 | 103.6 |
| (West) | 1332/225 | 104.3 |
| (Salisbury) |  | 103.5 |
| 33 Radio W. M. (West Midlands) | 1458/206 | 95.6 |
| (Sedgeley) | 828/362 | 95.6 |
| 34 Radio York (Central) | 666/450 | 103.7 |
| (East Coast) | 1260/238 | 95.5 |
| (North & NW) | 666/450 | 104.3 |
| ISLE OF MAN |  |  |
| 35 Manx Radio | 1368/219 | 96.9 |
|  | 1368/219 | 89.0 |

## INDEPENDENT LOCAL RADIO

Local radio stations giving road and weather reports

| M.W.kHz/metres | V.H.F. (Mhz) |  |
|---|---|---|
| 1 Beacon Radio (Wolverhampton & Black Country) | 990/303 | 97.2 |
| (Shrewsbury & Telford) | 990/303 | 103.1 |
| 2 B.R.M.B. Radio (Birmingham) | 1152/261 | 96.4 |
| 3 Capitol Radio (London) | 548/194 | 95.8 |
| 4 Chiltern Radio | 828/362 | 97.6 |
| (Bedford) | 792/379 | 96.9 |
| (Northampton) | 1557/193 | 96.9 |
| 5 Hereward Radio |  |  |
| 6 County Sound Radio (Guildford) | 1476/203 | 96.4 |
| 7 CH FM |  | 103 |
| 8 Devon Air Radio (Exeter) | 666/450 | 97.0 |
| (Torbay) | 954/314 | 96.4 |
| 9 Essex Radio (Southend) | 1431/210 | 96.3 |
| (Chelmsford) | 1359/220 | 102.6 |
| 10 Fox FM |  |  |
| (Oxford) |  | 102.6 |
| (Banbury) |  | 97.4 |
| 11 G.W.R. (Bath) |  | 103.0 |
| (Bristol) | 1260/238 | 96.3 |
| (Swindon) | 1161/258 | 97.2 |
| (West Wiltshire) | 936/321 | 102.6 |
| 12 Hereward Radio (Peterborough) | 1332/225 | 102.7 |
| 13 Horizon Radio |  |  |
| (Milton Keynes) |  | 103.3 |
| 14 Invicta Radio (Maidstone & Medway) | 1242/242 | 103.1 |
| (Ashford) | 603/497 | 96.1 |
| (Canterbury) | 603/497 | 102.8 |
| (Dover) | 603/497 | 97.0 |
| (Thanet) | 603/497 | 95.9 |
| 15 London Broadcasting Company | 1152/261 | 97.3 |
| 16 Leicester Sound | 1260/238 | 103.2 |
| 17 Marcher Sound (Wrexham & Deeside) | 1260/238 | 103.4 |
| 18 Mercia Sound (Coventry) | 1359/220 | 97.0 |
| 19 Metro Radio (Tyne & Wear) | 1152/261 | 97.1 |
| (Tyne Valley) |  | 103.0 |
| 20 Moray Firth Radio (Inverness) | 1107/271 | 97.4 |
| 21 North Sound Radio (Aberdeen) | 1035/290 | 96.9 |
| 22 Ocean Sound (Portsmouth) | 1170/257 | 97.5 |
| (Southampton) | 1557/193 | 103.2 |
| (Winchester) |  | 96.7 |
| 23 Orchard FM |  |  |
| (Taunton) |  | 102.6 |
| (Yeovil) |  | 97.1 |
| 24 Pennine Radio (Bradford) | 1278/235 | 97.5 |
| (Huddersfield & Halifax) | 1530/196 | 102.5 |
| 25 Piccadilly Radio (Manchester) | 1152/261 | 103.0 |
| 26 Plymouth Sound (Tavistock) | 1152/261 | 96.6 |
| (Plympton) | 1152/261 | 97.0 |
| 27 Radio Aire (Leeds) | 828/362 | 96.3 |
| 28 Radio Broadland (Great Yarmouth & Norwich) | 1152/260 | 102.4 |
| 29 Radio Borders |  |  |
| (Selkirk) |  | 96.8 |
| (Berwick) |  | 97.5 |
| (Peebles) |  | 103.1 |
| (Byemouth) |  | 103.4 |
| 30 Radio City (Liverpool) | 1548/194 | 96.7 |
| 31 Radio Clyde (Glasgow) | 1152/261 | 102.5 |
| 32 Radio Forth (Edinburgh) | 1548/194 | 97.3 |
| 33 Radio Hallam (Sheffield) | 1548/194 | 97.4 |
| (Rotherham) | 1548/194 | 96.1 |
| (Barnsley) | 1305/230 | 102.9 |
| (Doncaster) | 990/303 | 103.4 |
| 34 Radio Mercury (Reigate & Crawley) | 1521/197 | 102.7 |
| (Horsham) | 1521/197 | 97.5 |
| 35 Radio Orwell (Ipswich) | 1170/257 | 97.1 |
| 36 Radio Tay (Dundee) | 1161/258 | 102.8 |
| (Perth) | 1584/189 | 96.4 |
| 37 Radio Tees (Teeside) | 1170/257 | 96.6 |
| 38 Radio Trent (Nottingham) | 999/301 | 96.2 |
| (Derby) | 945/317 | 102.8 |
| 39 Radio 210 (Reading) | 1431/210 | 97.0 |
| (Basingstoke & Andover) | 1431/210 | 102.9 |
| 40 Radio Wyvern (Hereford) | 954/314 | 97.6 |
| (Worcester) | 1530/196 | 102.8 |
| 41 Red Dragon Radio (Cardiff) | 1359/221 | 103.2 |
| (Newport) | 1305/230 | 97.4 |
| 42 Red Rose Radio |  |  |
| (Preston & Blackpool) | 999/301 | 97.4 |
| 43 Saxon Radio (Bury St Edmunds) | 1251/240 | 96.4 |
| 44 Severn Sound (Gloucs & Chelt) | 774/388 | 102.4 |
| (Stroud) |  | 103.0 |
| 45 Signal Radio (Stoke-on-Trent) | 1170/257 | 102.6 |
| 46 South West Sound (Dumfries) |  | 97.2 |
| 47 Southern Sound (Brighton) | 1323/227 | 103.5 |
| (Newhaven) |  | 96.9 |
| (Eastbourne) |  | 102.4 |
| (Hastings) |  | 97.5 |
| 48 Swansea Sound | 1170/257 | 96.4 |
| 49 Two Counties Radio |  |  |
| (Bournemouth) | 828/362 | 102.3 |
| 50 Viking Radio (Humberside) | 1161/258 | 96.9 |
| 51 West Sound (Ayr) | 1035/290 | 96.7 |
| (Girvan) | 1035/290 | 97.5 |
| **NORTHERN IRELAND** |  |  |
| 52 Call FM (Belfast) |  | 92.4 |
| 53 Downtown Radio (Newtownards) | 102.6 | 96.4 |
|  |  | 102.4 |

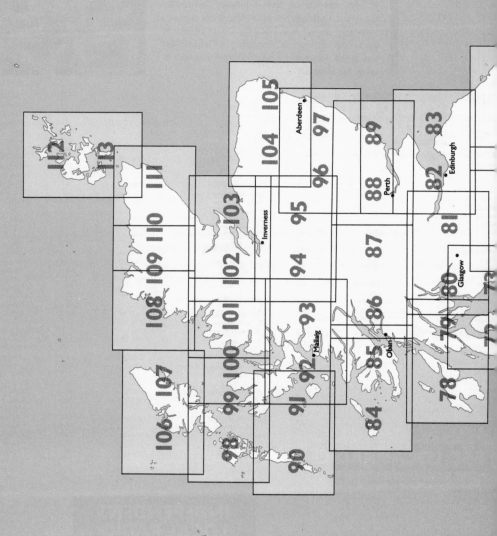

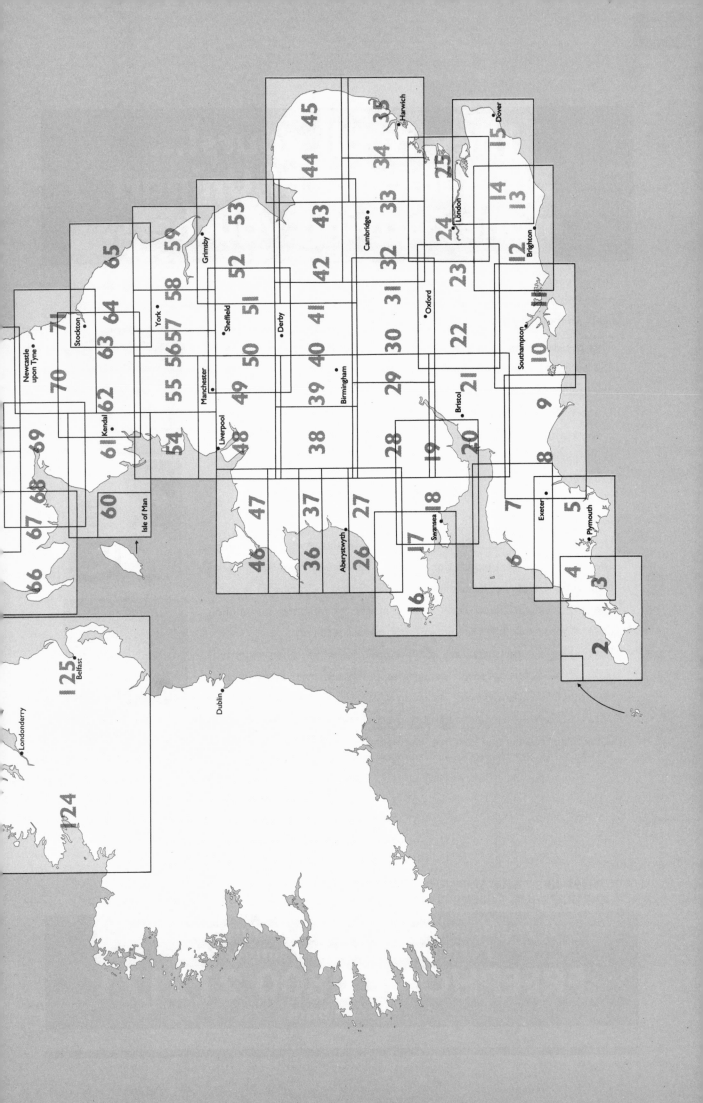

# They're all yours!...
# ...A selection of Unipart money-saving vouchers.

These vouchers enable you to enjoy discounts of between 25p and a huge £30.00! They are redeemable against a host of superb high quality products from brand names that are leaders in their fields, Unipart, Rover and UniqueAir.

### The products include :

The collectable 1992 Unipart Calendar

The useful 1992 Unipart Calendar Diary

Unipart's Samson Premium Battery with its unique guarantee: "You'll need a new car before you buy a new battery"

High quality Unipart Air and Oil Filters for ease of fitting and full engine protection

Unipart Surefire Performance Plus Spark Plugs with a dual copper core for improved performance

Unipart Surelife Wiper Blades – superior technology, superior wipe

The *New* range of Unipart Car Mats to suit all your individual needs

UniqueAir Carphone Installation – help is just a phone call away

The 1992 Unipart Road Atlas – an almanac of motoring information

Rover Approved Bulb Packs (available for all makes of car)

Rover Fire Extinguishers, an all-important item for safer motoring.

10% off all Rover approved accessories purchased from Rover dealers valued at £50.00 or over (RRP including VAT)

## HOW TO USE YOUR VOUCHERS

Cut out your coupon and take it to your nearest participating Unipart stockist for the Unipart products and your nearest Rover Dealer for the Rover products, and enjoy your discounts !

DEALER STAMP

**THESE ARE TRULY EXCEPTIONAL OFFERS, SO HURRY ALONG TO YOUR NEAREST PARTICIPATING STOCKIST! FOR REDEMPTION DATES SEE REVERSE OF VOUCHERS.**

### If you have any difficulty in finding your local Participating Stockist simply call

# FREEPHONE 0800 212171
## 8am - 8pm

## UNIPART

### £1 OFF A PACK OF 4 SUREFIRE PERFORMANCE PLUS SPARK PLUGS

VALID FROM 1st MAY TO 31st AUGUST 1991 ONLY
REDEEMABLE AT YOUR LOCAL UNIPART STOCKIST.

## UNIPART

### £2 OFF A UNIPART 1992 CALENDAR

VALID FROM 1st SEPTEMBER TO 31st OCTOBER 1991 ONLY
REDEEMABLE AT YOUR LOCAL UNIPART STOCKIST.

## UNIPART

### £3.00 OFF A SAMSON PREMIUM BATTERY

VALID FROM 1st OCTOBER TO 31st DECEMBER 1991 ONLY
REDEEMABLE AT YOUR LOCAL UNIPART STOCKIST.

## UNIPART

### 50p OFF A UNIPART 1992 ROAD ATLAS

VALID FROM 1st SEPTEMBER TO 31st OCTOBER 1991 ONLY
REDEEMABLE AT YOUR LOCAL UNIPART STOCKIST.

## UNIPART

### 25p OFF EITHER AN OIL FILTER OR AN AIR FILTER

VALID FROM 1st MAY TO 30th SEPTEMBER 1991 ONLY
REDEEMABLE AT YOUR LOCAL UNIPART STOCKIST.

## UNIPART

### £30 OFF THE INSTALLMENT OF A UNIQUEAIR CARPHONE

SEE REVERSE FOR DETAILS

## UNIPART

### £1 OFF A SET OF UNIPART CAR MATS OVER £10 RRP

VALID FROM 1st SEPTEMBER TO 30th NOVEMBER 1991 ONLY
REDEEMABLE AT YOUR LOCAL UNIPART STOCKIST.

## ROVER

### £2 OFF ROVER UNIVERSAL BULB KIT
#### AJM 2295

VALID FROM 1st MAY TO 31st DECEMBER 1991 REDEEMABLE AT ALL ROVER STOCKISTS.

## UNIPART

### 50p OFF UNIPART SURELIFE PLUS WIPER BLADES - TWIN PACK

VALID FROM 1st SEPTEMBER TO 30th NOVEMBER 1991 ONLY
REDEEMABLE AT YOUR LOCAL UNIPART STOCKIST.

## ROVER

### £5 OFF ROVER FIRE EXTINGUISHER
#### KDF 10002

VALID FROM 1st MAY TO 31st DECEMBER 1991 REDEEMABLE AT ALL ROVER STOCKISTS.

## UNIPART

### 50p OFF A UNIPART 1992 CALENDAR DIARY

VALID FROM 1st OCTOBER TO 30th NOVEMBER 1991 ONLY
REDEEMABLE AT YOUR LOCAL UNIPART STOCKIST.

## ROVER

### 10% OFF ALL ROVER APPROVED ACCESSORIES WHEN YOU SPEND £50 OR OVER (INC. VAT)

Part Number . . . . . . . . . . . .
VALID FROM 1st MAY TO 31st DECEMBER 1991 REDEEMABLE AT ALL ROVER STOCKISTS.

SEE REVERSE FOR DETAILS

## Row 1, Left

**UNIPART**

• NOT REDEEMABLE FOR CASH • ONE VOUCHER PER PURCHASE
• NOT TO BE USED IN CONJUNCTION WITH ANY OTHER OFFER
ON THIS PRODUCT

**TO THE RETAILER** This coupon will be redeemed by your local Unipart Wholesaler at full value, provided it has been accepted as part payment against the product stated overleaf. Coupons must be presented within two months of the consumer closing date. Unipart reserve the right to refuse redemption of defaced or damaged coupons or those which have not been validly redeemed!

SIGNATURE
NAME
ADDRESS
YOUR REGISTRATION NUMBER

## Row 1, Right

• NOT REDEEMABLE FOR CASH • ONE VOUCHER PER PURCHA
• NOT TO BE USED IN CONJUNCTION WITH ANY OTHER OFF
ON THIS PRODUCT

**TO THE RETAILER** This coupon will be redeemed by your local Unipart Wholesaler at full va provided it has been accepted as part payment against the product stated overleaf. Coupons must be presented within two months of the consumer closing date. Unipart reserve the right to refuse redemption of defaced or damaged coupons or those which have not been validly redeemed!

SIGNATURE
NAME
ADDRESS
YOUR REGISTRATION NUMBER

## Row 2, Left

**UNIPART**

• NOT REDEEMABLE FOR CASH • ONE VOUCHER PER PURCHASE
• NOT TO BE USED IN CONJUNCTION WITH ANY OTHER OFFER
ON THIS PRODUCT

**TO THE RETAILER** This coupon will be redeemed by your local Unipart Wholesaler at full value, provided it has been accepted as part payment against the product stated overleaf. Coupons must be presented within two months of the consumer closing date. Unipart reserve the right to refuse redemption of defaced or damaged coupons or those which have not been validly redeemed!

SIGNATURE
NAME
ADDRESS
YOUR REGISTRATION NUMBER

## Row 2, Right

**UNIPART**

• NOT REDEEMABLE FOR CASH • ONE VOUCHER PER PURCHA
• NOT TO BE USED IN CONJUNCTION WITH ANY OTHER OFFE
ON THIS PRODUCT

**TO THE RETAILER** This coupon will be redeemed by your local Unipart Wholesaler at full val provided it has been accepted as part payment against the product stated overleaf. Coupons mus presented within two months of the consumer closing date. Unipart reserve the right to refuse redemption of defaced or damaged coupons or those which have not been validly redeemed!

SIGNATURE
NAME
ADDRESS
YOUR REGISTRATION NUMBER

## Row 3, Left

**UNIPART**

• NOT REDEEMABLE FOR CASH • ONE VOUCHER PER PURCHASE
• NOT TO BE USED IN CONJUNCTION WITH ANY OTHER OFFER
ON THIS PRODUCT

**TO THE CONSUMER** This coupon will be redeemed when a uniqueair carphone is fitted to your vehicle. Contact UNIQUEAIR LTD., 26 Blacklands Way, Abingdon Business Park, Abingdon, Oxon. OX14 1DY or telephone (0235) 554883 for further information. The offer is valid provided it has been accepted as part payment against the product stated overleaf within the validity dates. UNIQUEAIR Ltd. reserve the right to refuse redemption of defaced or damaged coupons or those which have been validly redeemed.

SIGNATURE
NAME
ADDRESS
YOUR REGISTRATION NUMBER

## Row 3, Right

**UNIPART**

• NOT REDEEMABLE FOR CASH • ONE VOUCHER PER PURCHASE
• NOT TO BE USED IN CONJUNCTION WITH ANY OTHER OFFER
ON THIS PRODUCT

**TO THE RETAILER** This coupon will be redeemed by your local Unipart Wholesaler at full val provided it has been accepted as part payment against the product stated overleaf. Coupons must presented within two months of the consumer closing date. Unipart reserve the right to refuse redemption of defaced or damaged coupons or those which have not been validly redeemed!

SIGNATURE
NAME
ADDRESS
YOUR REGISTRATION NUMBER

## Row 4, Left

• NOT REDEEMABLE FOR CASH • ONE VOUCHER PER PURCHASE
• NOT TO BE USED IN CONJUNCTION WITH ANY OTHER OFFER
ON THIS PRODUCT

**TO THE RETAILER** This coupon will be redeemed by your local Unipart Wholesaler at full value, provided it has been accepted as part payment against the product stated overleaf. Coupons must be presented within two months of the consumer closing date. Unipart reserve the right to refuse redemption of defaced or damaged coupons or those which have not been validly redeemed!

SIGNATURE _____
NAME _____
ADDRESS _____
YOUR REGISTRATION NUMBER

## Row 4, Right

**UNIPART**

• NOT REDEEMABLE FOR CASH • ONE VOUCHER PER PURCHA
• NOT TO BE USED IN CONJUNCTION WITH ANY OTHER OFF
ON THIS PRODUCT

**TO THE RETAILER** This coupon will be redeemed by your local Unipart Wholesaler at full valu provided it has been accepted as part payment against the product stated overleaf. Coupons must presented within two months of the consumer closing date. Unipart reserve the right to refuse redemption of defaced or damaged coupons or those which have not been validly redeemed!

SIGNATURE
NAME
ADDRESS
YOUR REGISTRATION NUMBER

## Row 5, Left

• NOT REDEEMABLE FOR CASH • ONE VOUCHER PER PURCHASE
• NOT TO BE USED IN CONJUNCTION WITH ANY OTHER OFFER
ON THIS PRODUCT

**TO THE RETAILER** This coupon will be redeemed by your local Unipart Wholesaler at full value, provided it has been accepted as part payment against the product stated overleaf. Coupons must be presented within two months of the consumer closing date. Unipart reserve the right to refuse redemption of defaced or damaged coupons or those which have not been validly redeemed!

SIGNATURE _____
NAME _____
ADDRESS _____
YOUR REGISTRATION NUMBER

## Row 5, Right

**UNIPART**

• NOT REDEEMABLE FOR CASH • ONE VOUCHER PER PURCHASE
• NOT TO BE USED IN CONJUNCTION WITH ANY OTHER OFFER
ON THIS PRODUCT

**TO THE RETAILER** This coupon will be redeemed by your local Unipart Wholesaler at full valu provided it has been accepted as part payment against the product stated overleaf. Coupons must presented within two months of the consumer closing date. Unipart reserve the right to refuse redemption of defaced or damaged coupons or those which have not been validly redeemed!

SIGNATURE
NAME
ADDRESS
YOUR REGISTRATION NUMBER

## Row 6, Left

• NOT REDEEMABLE FOR CASH • ONE VOUCHER PER PURCHASE
• NOT TO BE USED IN CONJUNCTION WITH ANY OTHER OFFER
ON THIS PRODUCT

This offer applies only to products listed in the Accessory Salesman's Guide (MMM 9413). Part Number details of purchased products MUST be entered on the space on the front of this voucher.

**TO THE RETAILER** This coupon will be redeemed by your local Unipart Wholesaler at full value, provided it has been accepted as part payment against the product stated overleaf. Coupons must be presented within two months of the consumer closing date. Unipart reserve the right to refuse redemption of defaced or damaged coupons or those which have not been validly redeemed!

SIGNATURE _____
NAME _____
ADDRESS _____
YOUR REGISTRATION NUMBER

## Row 6, Right

**UNIPART**

• NOT REDEEMABLE FOR CASH • ONE VOUCHER PER PURCHASE
• NOT TO BE USED IN CONJUNCTION WITH ANY OTHER OFFER
ON THIS PRODUCT

**TO THE RETAILER** This coupon will be redeemed by your local Unipart Wholesaler at full valu provided it has been accepted as part payment against the product stated overleaf. Coupons must presented within two months of the consumer closing date. Unipart reserve the right to refuse redemption of defaced or damaged coupons or those which have not been validly redeemed!

SIGNATURE
NAME
ADDRESS
YOUR REGISTRATION NUMBER

# SAFER MOTORING

Vehicles today are more reliable than they have ever been and regular servicing and maintenance can do a lot to ensure your continued safety on the roads.

However, breakdowns happen to someone every hour of every day so, in conjunction with the Thames Valley Police, Unipart offer the following advice for your safety, in the case of your finding yourself stranded:

If you have broken down, make sure it is safe to get out. Quickly move the car to the side of the road. If you are on a motorway pull over to the hard shoulder.

Keep in mind the danger of passing traffic. Switch on the hazard warning and side lights. Consider placing a warning triangle behind the car, but remember a stationary vehicle on the hard shoulder of a motorway can be struck by other vehicles—it is not a safe place to be.

Telephone for assistance. Clearly state your name. If you are female and driving alone, emphasise this fact; all the major motoring organisations give priority to lone females. If a vehicle stops near and lingers suspiciously, drop the phone (do not replace it on the hook), get inside your car and lock all the doors. Remember, the emergency motorway telephones are on a direct line to the police who will be able to get you assistance.

*With crime on the increase, lone female drivers, elderly and disabled drivers may feel particularly vulnerable.* In these circumstances you may prefer to put on the hazard lights, stay locked in the car and wait for help. However, there is no guarantee how long you may have to wait. If someone approaches the car, ask them to phone the police for you.

Should someone approach to offer help, do not unlock the door or open your window. Ask that person to phone for help. Should this person's actions arouse suspicion, take the registration number. It is a good idea to install a car

telephone or even have a replica mobile phone to discourage people. Ring the police on 999 if anyone looking suspicious approaches your car. Describe the vehicle and the person.

When official help arrives, open the window far enough to ask for identification. No one from the emergency breakdown services should mind identifying themselves.

### General Advice

Make sure you check your oil and water regularly. Check

that your spare tyre is roadworthy and that you have a jack that works. If you don't already know how, practise changing a wheel in your own time—be prepared for that cold winter's day, stranded on the hard shoulder of the motorway. Do not let small repairs or problems with starting , for example, go unattended. They won't get better by themselves and could let you down at the worst time!

**Always carry a torch, blanket, free standing hazard light, warning triangle and jump leads. Apart from saving the day in an emergency, they will give you considerably more peace of mind in your daily motoring.**

# HOW TO SAVE PETROL

Saving petrol is a major part of efficient motoring, all the more so in these cost-conscious days. In association with the RAC, Unipart have therefore produced this comprehensive guide to getting the most out of motoring. After years of experience of 'Cutting the Cost of Motoring', we believe we're well-qualified to help you make genuine economies.

### Drive Carefully!

The most substantial fuel economy you can make is by driving your car effectively, which means anticipation, timing and skilful use of controls. The efficient use of the accelerator and gears is what will cut your fuel bills most. Even if you're a highly experienced driver, reading the points listed below might refresh your memory and have a distinctly beneficial effect on your next petrol bill.

### Starting Up

At this point a car uses much more petrol than it does to maintain a constant speed. Do not use the starter in short bursts as it could damage the flywheel, but don't leave it on so long that it runs the battery flat. If the engine does not start after 10 seconds, wait 20 seconds before trying again.

### Using the Choke (where fitted)

It is most economical to warm up the engine on the move, but if you do this while stationary, remember to gradually reduce the choke as a prolonged over-rich mixture wastes petrol. Never rev the engine when first started. Fast starts and high revving in each gear uses up to 50 per cent more petrol than a smooth start and a steady progression through the gears.

### Speed

For the average 2 litre car, petrol consumption is twice as heavy when driving at a steady speed of 70mph compared to driving at 30mph. It is more economical to accelerate quietly, even though it takes longer to reach the speed you want. Best economic performance, when a car reaches maximum torque, is usually around 2000 - 3000 rpm at a road speed of 40-60 mph.

### Safe and Economic Cornering

Anticipation, gradual braking and minimum use of gears saves petrol. Only one gear change should be necessary once the car has decelerated to a suitable speed, unless you are following a series of bends or a particularly acute corner.

### Braking: Thinking Ahead Saves Petrol

Anticipate the need to stop well ahead, so you can slow your car simply by taking your foot off the accelerator. This will also reduce wear on brakes and tyres

### Gearing for Efficiency

Timing is critical. The right moment to change up a gear is when the speed you have reached can be maintained in the next gear, without pressing down on the accelerator. The best time to change down is when you can do so without causing a noisy, racing surge in the engine speed. A rev counter is a good guide for the best time to change gears. For best results, keep engine speed at maximum torque. If you don't have one, find out from your handbook what maximum speeds the manufacturer recommends for each gear. Optimum fuel efficiency is obtained by changing gears at half the recommended maximum speed for each gear. For example, if 50mph is the given maximum speed for 3rd gear, change up from and down to 2nd gear at 25mph.

### Hills

The best plan is to build up speed beforehand and maintain it without accelerating in a lower gear. However don't stay in a high gear too long when driving uphill. Avoid peak revs in each gear, over-revving the engine can cause damage.

### 5th Gear

Although 5th gear is intended to give optimal fuel economy when cruising at high speeds, remember that changing too soon can waste petrol.

### Automatics

Cars fitted with automatic gearboxes can be driven nearly as economically as cars with manual transmission. There is a large advantage to be gained in heavy traffic where stop and start conditions are experienced. However, fuel consumption will be affected if excessive use is made of the "kick down" facility that is fitted to all automatic gearboxes.

### Fuel Economy for Traffic Conditions

City rush hour traffic is twice as expensive as driving on main road conditions, while motorway driving can increase costs by more than one third! Good route-planning and choosing a quiet time to make your journey are essential to obtaining the best economic performance from your car.

### Traffic Jams

It is much more efficient to keep moving very slowly than to stop and start. Let the traffic get ahead; you will gain nothing by rushing to catch up. Remember how much extra petrol it takes to start up again! It's worth bearing in mind that driving quietly not only saves petrol—it can save you from the effects of stress!

### Inefficient Short Journeys

Drivers who use their cars for short journeys pay more. Even on uncongested roads you can expect fuel consumption in the first 3 miles to be twice the rate of normal driving. Where possible, it makes sense to avoid short trips to the shops or school for example, when you could walk or cycle and make better environmental sense into the bargain!

IMPECCABLE DRIVING WON'T SAVE YOU ANYTHING HOWEVER, IF YOUR CAR IS STRUGGLING ALONG WITH WORN OR FAULTY PARTS. One malfunctioning part will throw the whole system out of joint and bring extra, damaging pressure to bear on it.

**Here's the first thing to avoid:** The most obvious economy measures may at first seem to be on 'non-essential' maintenance, but if these neglect the need for maintaining efficient engine performance they will be

false economies:

### reduced economy = higher fuel consumption = **increased costs**

In the engine's original design, individual components were carefully specified so that they matched and complemented each other's performance and produced the optimum combination of power, 'driveability' and overall economy.

Major deviations from that original component specification invariably create imbalances which, in affecting the engine's performance, have a direct impact on fuel economy.

**Unipart offer the UK's widest range of premium quality parts. Here are just a few reasons why you should make sure you fit only quality parts to get the best out of your car:**

### Air filters

Running with a clogged filter can easily cause up to 10% increase in fuel consumption. The right filter should also maintain the most efficient balance of air to fuel.

### Spark Plugs

The correct spark plug is vital to optimum performance and fuel economy: assists cold starting, minimises damaging corrosion and maintains peak engine performance for longer. Spark Plugs work best if all the other ignition components are in good condition.

### Thermostats and Radiator Caps

Remember: a defective thermostat could mean you having to use the choke for longer than necessary, resulting directly in fuel wastage or at the other end of the scale, overheating! Overheating could also be caused by a defective radiator cap; most modern engines operate with high coolant pressure and it is

essential that the correct pressure is used.

### Oil

Oil lubricates the moving parts of your engine, stops it seizing and carries away heat; most oils are multigrade and tend to maintain viscosity with temperature, so the correct specification is essential for ultimate performance. Never allow the oil level to drop below the recommended point, but, equally, don't overfill it as this can cause considerable engine damage.

### Exhausts

Beware cheap imitation exhausts; just because they fit and look right from the outside doesn't mean they will do the job they are meant to i.e. extract the burnt gases away from the cylinders in a controlled manner.

### Carburation

Adjusting the mixture of air to fuel to make the engine 'run lean' will not save on fuel. The right mixture of air and fuel is the one originally specified by the manufacturers when the engine was designed. Any attempt to weaken the mixture could result in expensive damage. Modern vehicles and those fitted with fuel injection will require specialist equipment to accurately set the fuel mixture.

**No matter what car you drive today, you can always get a little more performance and a little more economy from it simply by paying attention to the points discussed in this leaflet—choosing quality parts like Unipart. Take care of your car in the garage and on the road and it will take care of you.**

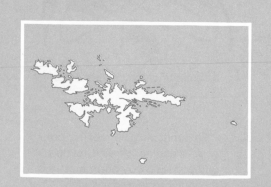

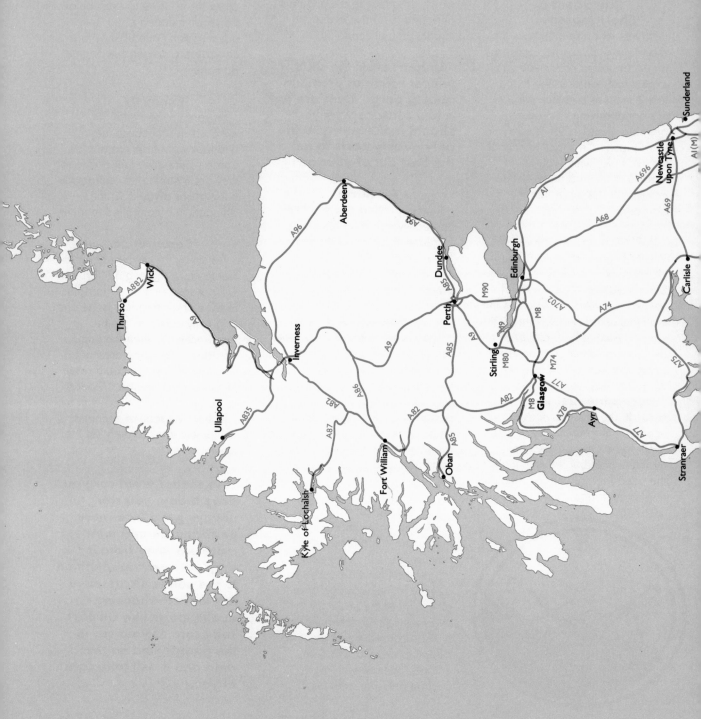

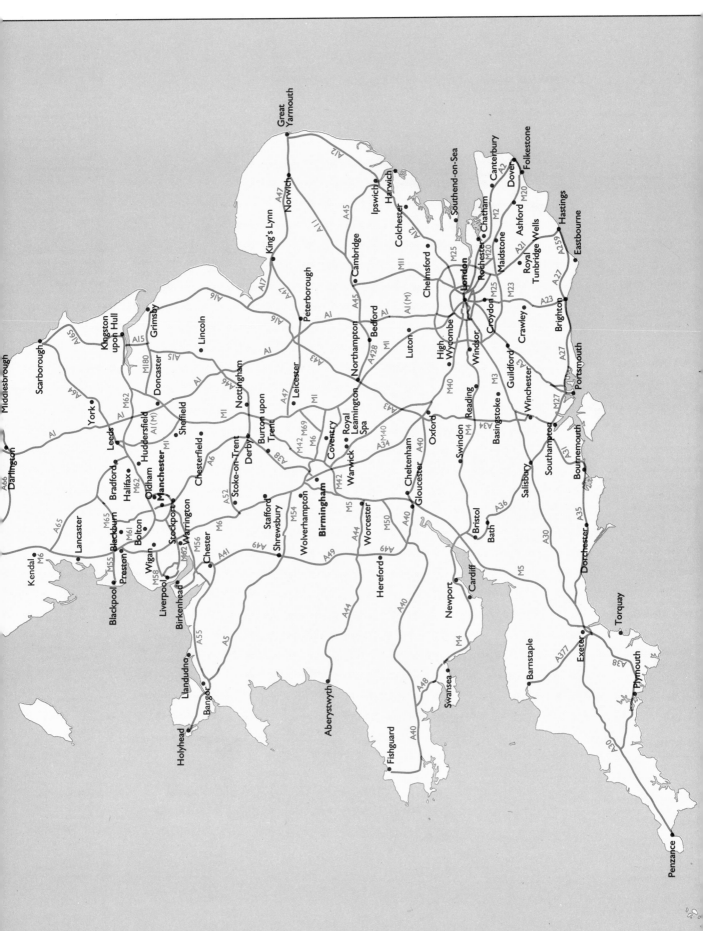

25  50  75  100 km

25

50 mls

# WEATHER HAZARDS

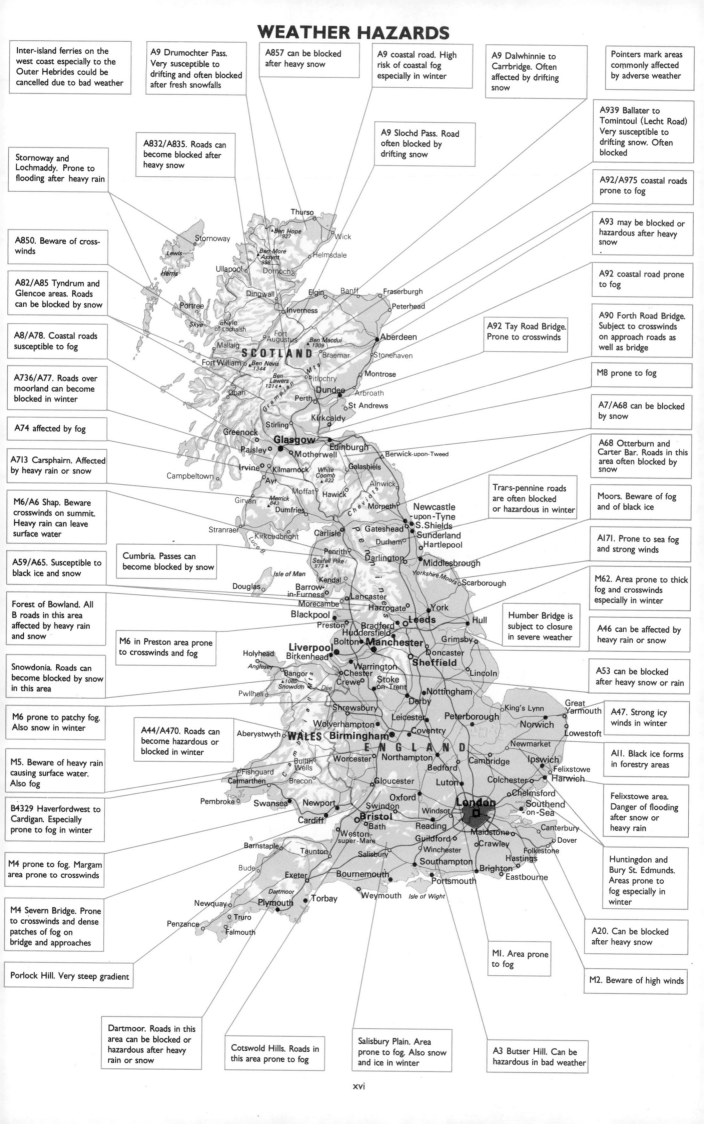

Inter-island ferries on the west coast especially to the Outer Hebrides could be cancelled due to bad weather

A9 Drumochter Pass. Very susceptible to drifting and often blocked after fresh snowfalls

A857 can be blocked after heavy snow

A9 coastal road. High risk of coastal fog especially in winter

A9 Dalwhinnie to Carrbridge. Often affected by drifting snow

Pointers mark areas commonly affected by adverse weather

A832/A835. Roads can become blocked after heavy snow

A9 Slochd Pass. Road often blocked by drifting snow

A939 Ballater to Tomintoul (Lecht Road) Very susceptible to drifting snow. Often blocked

Stornoway and Lochmaddy. Prone to flooding after heavy rain

A92/A975 coastal roads prone to fog

A850. Beware of cross-winds

A93 may be blocked or hazardous after heavy snow

A82/A85 Tyndrum and Glencoe areas. Roads can be blocked by snow

A92 coastal road prone to fog

A8/A78. Coastal roads susceptible to fog

A90 Forth Road Bridge. Subject to crosswinds on approach roads as well as bridge

A736/A77. Roads over moorland can become blocked in winter

A92 Tay Road Bridge. Prone to crosswinds

M8 prone to fog

A74 affected by fog

A7/A68 can be blocked by snow

A713 Carsphairn. Affected by heavy rain or snow

A68 Otterburn and Carter Bar. Roads in this area often blocked by snow

M6/A6 Shap. Beware crosswinds on summit. Heavy rain can leave surface water

Trans-pennine roads are often blocked or hazardous in winter

Moors. Beware of fog and of black ice

A59/A65. Susceptible to black ice and snow

Cumbria. Passes can become blocked by snow

A171. Prone to sea fog and strong winds

Forest of Bowland. All B roads in this area affected by heavy rain and snow

M62. Area prone to thick fog and crosswinds especially in winter

Humber Bridge is subject to closure in severe weather

A46 can be affected by heavy rain or snow

M6 in Preston area prone to crosswinds and fog

Snowdonia. Roads can become blocked by snow in this area

A53 can be blocked after heavy snow or rain

M6 prone to patchy fog. Also snow in winter

A47. Strong icy winds in winter

A44/A470. Roads can become hazardous or blocked in winter

M5. Beware of heavy rain causing surface water. Also fog

A11. Black ice forms in forestry areas

B4329 Haverfordwest to Cardigan. Especially prone to fog in winter

Felixstowe area. Danger of flooding after snow or heavy rain

M4 prone to fog. Margam area prone to crosswinds

Huntingdon and Bury St. Edmunds. Areas prone to fog especially in winter

M4 Severn Bridge. Prone to crosswinds and dense patches of fog on bridge and approaches

A20. Can be blocked after heavy snow

Porlock Hill. Very steep gradient

M1. Area prone to fog

M2. Beware of high winds

Dartmoor. Roads in this area can be blocked or hazardous after heavy rain or snow

Cotswold Hills. Roads in this area prone to fog

Salisbury Plain. Area prone to fog. Also snow and ice in winter

A3 Butser Hill. Can be hazardous in bad weather

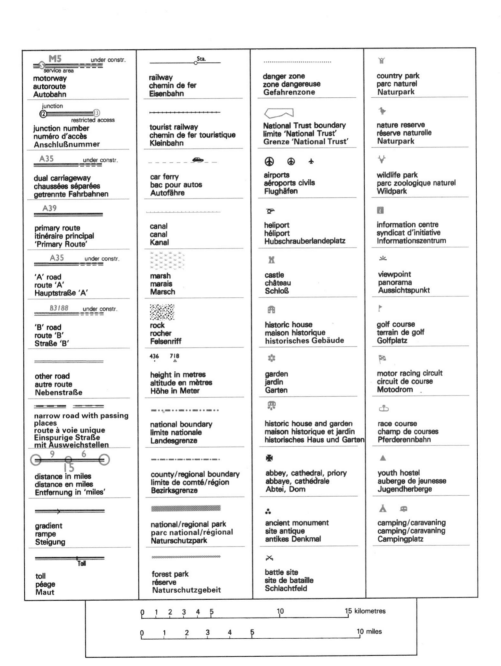

| | | | |
|---|---|---|---|
| **M5** service area under constr. | **Sta.** | danger zone | country park |
| motorway autoroute Autobahn | railway chemin de fer Eisenbahn | danger zone zone dangereuse Gefahrenzone | country park parc naturel Naturpark |
| junction ② ③ restricted access | | | |
| junction number numéro d'accès Anschlußnummer | tourist railway chemin de fer touristique Kleinbahn | National Trust boundary limite 'National Trust' Grenze 'National Trust' | nature reserve réserve naturelle Naturpark |
| A35 under constr. | | | |
| dual carriageway chaussées séparées getrennte Fahrbahnen | car ferry bac pour autos Autofähre | airports aéroports civils Flughäfen | wildlife park parc zoologique naturel Wildpark |
| A39 | | | |
| primary route itinéraire principal 'Primary Route' | canal canal Kanal | heliport héliport Hubschrauberlandeplatz | information centre syndicat d'initiative Informationszentrum |
| A35 under constr. | | | |
| 'A' road route 'A' Hauptstraße 'A' | marsh marais Marsch | castle château Schloß | viewpoint panorama Aussichtspunkt |
| B3188 under constr. | | | |
| 'B' road route 'B' Straße 'B' | rock rocher Felsenriff | historic house maison historique historisches Gebäude | golf course terrain de golf Golfplatz |
| | 436 718 | | |
| other road autre route Nebenstraße | height in metres altitude en mètres Höhe in Meter | garden jardin Garten | motor racing circuit circuit de course Motodrom |
| narrow road with passing places route à voie unique Einspurige Straße mit Ausweichstellen | national boundary limite nationale Landesgrenze | historic house and garden maison historique et jardin historisches Haus und Garten | race course champ de courses Pferderennbahn |
| 9 6 15 | | | |
| distance in miles distance en miles Entfernung in 'miles' | county/regional boundary limite de comté/région Bezirksgrenze | abbey, cathedral, priory abbaye, cathédrale Abtei, Dom | youth hostel auberge de jeunesse Jugendherberge |
| gradient rampe Steigung | national/regional park parc national/régional Naturschutzpark | ancient monument site antique antikes Denkmal | camping/caravaning camping/caravaning Campingplatz |
| Toll | | | |
| toll péage Maut | forest park réserve Naturschutzgebiet | battle site site de bataille Schlachtfeld | |

0 1 2 3 4 5 10 15 kilometres

0 1 2 3 4 5 10 miles

0 1 2 3 4 5    10    15 kilometres
0 1 2 3 4 5    10 miles

**a**    **b**    **c**    **D**    **E**

**I**    Continuation westward on the same scale    **I**

Seven Stones

**2**    White Island    **2**
St Helen's    St Martin's
Bryher    Tean    Higher Town
Tresco
Eastern
Samson    Isles
North West Channel    The Road    Crow Sound
A3110
Hugh Town    St Mary's    To Penzance    **2**
The Garrison    Scilly Isles
A3112
Crim Rocks    St Mary's Sound    Towan
Broad Sound    Annet    Gugh Sound    **ISLES OF SCILLY**    Fistral    Newq
**3**    Bishop Rock    Smith Sound    St Agnes    Kelsey Head    Pentire
Western    West Pentire
Rocks    Holywell
Bay
Penhale Point    Holywell
Ligger Point    Cubert
Ligger    Penhale    Mo
or    Sands
Perran Bay
Bawden Rocks    Perranporth    Rose
or
Man and his man    Bolingey
Trevellas    Perranz
St Agnes Head    St Agnes    Penhallo
Mithian
**A**    **B**    Goonbell    Callestick
Mount    Tregavethan
Porthtowan    Hawke
Mawla    Blackwater    A3
Portreath    Scorr    Chacewater    Thr
Crane Islands    St Day    Cross Lanes    Bald
**4**    Godrevy Island    Navax Point    Illogan    Redruth    Twelveheads    Bisso
Coombe    Pool    Tuckingmill    Carnmenellis    Carnmarth
Gwithian    Kehelland    Carn Brea    Gwennap
Carbis Bay    Roseworthy    Camborne    Lanner    Four Lanes    Perranwell Sta
St Ives    Connor Downs    Barripper    Penhalvean    Perranarworthal
The Island    St Ives Bay    Phillack    Troon    Ponsanooth
Carn Naun Point    Halsetown    Angarrack    Hayle    Gwinear    Rosewarne    Praze-an-    Stithians    Penr
The Carracks    Trendrine    Towednack    Carnhell    Beeble    Pen
Gurnard's Head    Zennor    Hill    Trencrom    Lelant    Green    Crowan Beacon    Long
Porthmeor    Hill    Cripplesease    St Erth    Downs
Amalebra    Canonstown    Praze    Leedstown    Rame    Mabe
Pendeen Watch    Crowan    Porkellis    Edgcumbe    Burnthouse
Lower Boscaswell    Morvah    Newmill    St Erth    Townshend    Budock    Falmou
Trewellard    Bojewyan    Ludgvan    Relubbus    Godolphin    Nancegollan    Treverva    Water
Pendeen    Madron    Crowlas    Cross    Wendron    Penjerrick
Botallack    Carnyorth    Newbridge    Gulval    Longrock    St Hilary    Crowntown    Seworgan    Constantine
Cape Cornwall    St Just    Heamoor    Marazion    Goldsithney    Trescowe    Brill    Porth Navas    Smith
The Brisons    Bosavern    Tremethick Cross    Penzance    St Michael's    Germoe    Sithney    GLENDURGAN
Kelynack    Sancreed    Buryas    Chyandour    Mount    Perranuthnoe    Ashton    Tregonning    Helston    Gweek    Mawnan
Brane    Bridge    Newlyn    Hill    Mawgan    Helford    St A
Drift    Catchall    Rinsey    Breage    Garras    Constantine
Whitesand    Clows-an-wra    Mousehole    Praa Sands    Porthleven    Porthallow
Bay    Kerris    St Clement's Isle    Cudden Point    Loe    Newtown    Tregidden
Sennen Cove    Paul    Trewavas Head    Pool    St Keverne
Longships    Sennen    Mount's Bay    Gunwalloe    Mawgan    St Martin's    Traboe
**6**    Land's End    Trevescan    St Buryan    Boleigh    Berepper    Green
Porthcurno    Treen    Cury    Goonhilly
St Levan    Cribba Head    Lamorna Cove    Poldhu Cove    Downs    Cove
Gwennap Head    Logan Rock    Poldhu Point    Mullion
Runnel Stone    Porth Mellin    Gwenter
Mullion Cove
Mullion Island    Ruan Major    Black He
**7**    To Isles of Scilly    Predannack    Ruan Minor
Wollas    Cadgwith
Vellan Head    Grade
Toll    Landewednack
Kynance Cove    Hot Point
Lizard    Lizard Point

**A**    **B**    **C**    **D**    **E**

**6**

0 1 2 3 4 5    10    15 kilometres
0 1 2 3 4 5      10 miles

A    B    C    D    E

B R I S

**1**

**2**

North West Point
*Lundy*
(NT)
Shutter Point   Rat Island

Widmouth Head   Combe Martin Bay
**Ilfracombe**   Co
Lee Bay   Hele
Bull Point   Lee   Slade   Berrynarbor
Rockham Bay   Mortehoe   Sterridge
Morte Point
Woolacombe   Trimstone
*Morte Bay*   West Down
Pickwell   North   Bittadon   East D
Baggy Point   Buckland
Georgeham   Milltown
*Croyde Bay*   Croyde   Knowle   Halsinger   Muddifor
Saunton   Marwood   Youlston
*Saunton Sands*   Pippacott   Prixford   MARWOOD HILL   Kingsheanton
**Braunton**   Heanton   Ashford
Wrafton   Punchardon
*Braunton*   Toll
*Burrows*

**3**

*B A R N S T A P L E*

*O R*

*B I D E F O R D   B A Y*

The Neck
NORTHAM BURROWS
**Barns**
Bickington   Newpo
Pilton
Fremington   Landkey
Bickleton
Instow   A39
Appledore   Tapeley
Westward Ho!   Westleigh   Tawstock
St John's Chapel   Bishop
**Northam**   Westleigh   Tawto
Eastleigh   Newton Tracey
**Bideford**   East-the-Water   Loveacott
Abbotsham   Horwood   Ensis

**4**

Hartland Point
Titchberry
Windbury Point
Gallantry Bower
Hartland Quay   Clovelly
*Clovelly Bay*   Fairy Cross   Ford   Hiscott   Fishley Barton
Stoke   Hartland   Dyke   Buck's Mills   Yeo Vale   Landcross   Alverdiscott
Milford   Clovelly Cross   Buck's   Horns Cross   Gammaton Moor   Yarnscombe   Langrie
Philham   Cross   Goldworthy   Littleham   Woodtown   Huntshaw Cross
Elmscott   Tosberry   Cranford   Parkham   Parkham   Weare Giffard   Sherwood Green
Edistone   Ash   Buckland   Monkleigh   High Bullen
Woolfardisworthy   Almiston   Brewer   Frithelstock   **Great**
South Hole   Cross   Melbury   Frithelstock   **Torrington**   St Giles
Stone   in the Wood
Welcombe   Ashmansworthy   Powler's Piece   Taddiport   Kingscott
Meddon   Kismeblon   Little   ROSEMOOR   Roboro
*Torridge*   Northmoor   Bridge   Torrington

**5**

Gooseham   East Putford   Villavin
Morwenstow   Eastcott   Youlstone   Dinworthy   West Putford   Langtree   Beaford
*Higher Sharpnose Point*   Shop   Bradworthy   Bulkworthy   Stibb Cross   Winswell
*Lower Sharpnose Point*   Woodford   Brendon   Abbots   Peters Marland   Heanton   Dolto
*Upper Tamar Lake*   Bickington   Woolaton   Merton   Satchville
Coombe   Taylors Cross   Sutcombe   Newton St Petrock   Huish
Kilkhampton   Alfardisworthy   Milton Damerel   Dowlar
*Lower Tamar Lake*   *Waldon*   North Town
Stibb   Soldon Cross   Shebbear   Buckland   Petrockstowe
Rhude Cross   Youldonmoor   Thornbury   Filleigh   Ash   Meeth   Iddesle

**6**

Poughill
STAMFORD HILL
*Bude*   Flexbury   Grimscott   Youldon   Holsworthy   Bradford   Sheepwash   Hele Bridge
**Bude**   **Stratton**   Launcells   Beacon   Black   Monkokehampton
*Bay*   Cross   Chilsworthy   Torrington
Launcells   Pancrasweek   Cookbury   Basset's Cross
Red Post   **Holsworthy**   Anvil Corner   Brandis   Highampton   Hatherleigh
Helebridge   Marhamchurch   Rydon   Corner   Lydacott
Bridgerule   Pyworthy   Chasty   Hollacombe   Dunsland Cross
Widemouth Bay   Graddon Moor
Coppathorne   Titson   Yeomadon   *Graddon Moor*
*Halwill Forest*   Jacobstow

**7**

*Dizzard Point*
Poundstock   Tinney   Herdicott   Halwill Junction
Tregole   Trewint   Coffcott   Clawton   Halwill   Beaworthy   Northlew   Inwardleigh
St Gennys   Green   Quoditch   Upcott   Oaki   Folly Gate
Crackington Haven   Whitstone   North   Tetcott   Ashbury
*Cambeak*   Week St Mary   Tamerton   Ashwater   *Broadbury*
Wainhouse   Trebarrow   Lana   Henford   Germansweek   Southcott
Crackington   Corner   Luffincott   Yellands
*Fire Beacon Point*   Jacobstow   West Curry   Ashwater   Boasley Cross   Hewton
Tresparrett   South   Northcott   Virginstow
Posts   Collamoor Head   Wheatley   Maxworthy   Clubworthy   Boyton   East Panson   Bratton   Meldon   Yes Tor
**Boscastle**   Langdon   Caudworthy   Clovelly   Sou
Marshgate   Canworthy Water   Troswell   Bennacott   DANGE
Otterham   Warbstow   Brazacott   Bridestowe
Lesnewth   Renwenham   Bridgetown   Broadwoodwidger   Bridestowe   621...
ossiney   Tremaine   th Petherwin   Polapit Tamar   Cross Green   Bridestowe and Sourton
Ladycross

A    B    C    D    E

Scale: 0 1 2 3 4 5 ... 10 ... 15 kilometres / 0 1 2 3 4 5 ... 10 miles

A 20    B    C    D    E

Tytherington   Corton   Codford St Mary   Fisherton de la Mere   Winterbourne Stoke   West Amesbury   Wilsford   Newton Toney   Palestine   Fullerton

Codford St Peter   Boyton   Deptford   Berwick St James   Lake   Allington   Boscombe   Over Wallop   Middle Wallop   Nether Wallop   Longstock

Sherrington   Stockton   Wylye   Steeple Langford   Upper Woodford   Great Durnford   Idmiston   Lopcombe Corner   King's Somborne   Little Somborne

Great Ridge   Hanging Langford   Stapleford   Heale House (NT)   Netton   Porton   Winterslow   The Common   Whiteshoot Hill   Broughton   Houghton   Bossington   Horsebridge

1   Little Langford   Great Wishford   Stoford   Middle Woodford   Lower Woodford   Winterbourne Gunner   Winterbourne Dauntsey (NT)   Middle Winterslow   West Winterslow

Berwick St Leonard   Fonthill Bishop   Chilmark   Teffont Magna (NT)   Dinton   Baverstock   Fugglestone St Peter   Winterbourne Earls   Pitton

Hindon   Fonthill Gifford   Ridge   Teffont Evias   Barford St Martin   Burcombe   WILTON   Quidhampton   SALISBURY   Laverstock   West Tytherley   Brook

East Knoyle   Newtown   Tisbury   Sutton Mandeville   Fovant   Compton Chamberlayne   Netherhampton   Harnham   Farley   East Grimstead   West Dean   East Tytherley   Mottisfont   Michelmersh

Hatch   Swallowcliffe   Stratford Tony   Blyford   Alderbury   West Grimstead   Dean Hill   Carter's Clay   Kent's Oak   Timsbury

Semley   Ansty   Bishopstone   Coombe Bissett   Odstock   Whaddon Bodenham   Nunton   (NT)   Newtown   Awbridge   Stanbridge Earls   Romsey

2   Donhead St Andrew   White Sheet Hill   Fifield Bavant   Broad Chalke   Homington   Odstock Down   Charlton   Whiteparish   Sherfield English   East Wellow

Melbury Abbas (NT)   Ludwell   Berwick St John   Ebbesborne Wake   Mead End   Bowerchalke   Wick Down   Rockbourne Down   Wick   Downton   Morgan's Vale   Redlynch   Hamptworth   West Wellow   BROADLANDS   North Baddesley

Compton Abbas   Charlton   Woodminton   Woodfalls   Landford   Plaitford

Fontmell Magna   Woodyates   Martin Drove End   Whitsbury   BREAMORE   Hale   North Charford   Nomansland   Canada   OWER

Sutton Waldron   Ashmore   Deanland   Martin   Tidpit   Rockbourne   Upper Street   Breamore   Woodgreen   Deadman Hill   Bramshaw   Newbridge   Copythorne   Calmore   Totton

3   Tollard Royal   Sixpenny Handley   Pentridge   West Park   Damerham   Upper Burgate   Godshill   Fritham   Brook   Cadnam   Bartley   Netley Marsh   SO

Iwerne Minster   Woodcutts   Pentridge Hill   Boveridge   Sandleheath   Fordingbridge   Blissford   Stoney Cross   Woodlands   Hounsdown   Ashurst   Colbury

Fontmell Magna   Farnham   Monkton Up Wimborne   Cranborne   Ashford   Frogham   Newtown   Elim

Stubhampton   Minchington   Cashmoor   Wimborne St Giles   Edmondsham   Daggons   Alderholt   Stuckton   Hungerford   Gorley

Tarrant Gunville   Chettle   Gussage St Michael   Bickton   Harbridge   Linwood   Bolderwood   Emery Down   Lyndhurst Rd Sta.

Tarrant Hinton   Long Crichel   Gussage All Saints   Sutton Holms   Romford   Ibsley   THE   Bank   LYNDHURST

Pimperne Down   Moor Crichel   Knowlton   Whitmore   Verwood   Ringwood Forest   Moyles Court   NEW   Newtown

4   Tarrant Launceston   Tarrant Monkton   Manswood   Woodlands   Horton   Three Legged Cross   Ellingham   Linford   FOREST   Beaulieu Rd Sta.

Blandford Camp   Chalbury Common   Horton Common   Blashford   Poulner   Picket Post   FOREST   Brockenhurst

Tarrant Rawston   Witchampton   Hinton Martell   Uppington   Mannington   Ashley Heath   Ringwood   Burley Street   Burley

Charlton Marshall   Tarrant Keyneston   Gaunt's Common   Holt Heath   St Ives   St Leonards   Avon Castle   Burley Lodge   Bisterne Close   Balmerlawn

Tarrant Rushton   Langton Blandford   Stanbridge   Holt   Kingston   Bisterne   Setley

Thornicombe   Tarrant Crawford   Spetisbury   Tadden   Clapgate   Broom Hill   Trickett's Cross   Avon   Thorney Hill   Wootton   Sway   Tiptoe   Pilley Bailey

5   Sturminster Marshall   Pamphill   Colehill   Canford Bottom   Stapehill   Ferndown   Ripley   Shirley   Bransgore   Bashley   Boldre   Portmore

Anderson   Winterborne Zelston   Almer   WIMBORNE MINSTER   Hampreston   Dudsbury   Longham   Parley Cross   Sopley   Neacroft   Hinton   New Milton   Hordle   Walhampton   LYMINGTON

Morden   East Morden   Lytchett Matravers   East End   Canford Magna   West Parley   Hurn   MACPENNY'S   Admiral   Pier Sta.

Oxworth   Corfe Mullen   Bearwood   Canford Heath   Kinson   Moordown   Winkton   Holdenhurst   Burton   Highcliffe   Everton   Lower Pennington

Wareham Forest   Broadstone   Beacon Hill   Wallisdown   Newtown   Winton   Pokesdown   Wick   Barton on Sea   Lymore   Keyhaven   Milford on Sea

Slepe   Lytchett Minster   Upton   UPTON PARK   Longfleet   Branksome   Westbourne   Boscombe   Southbourne   CHRISTCHURCH   Mudeford

Wareham   POOLE   Parkstone   Branksome Park   BOURNEMOUTH   Christchurch Bay   Hengistbury Head

6   Stoborough   Arne   Lilliput   Canford Cliffs   Poole Bay   HURST CASTLE   FORT VICTORIA   Colwell Bay   Norton Green   Freshwater

Stokeford   Ridge   Poole Harbour   Brownsea Island   Sandbanks   The Needles   Totland   Easton

DANGER   Stoborough Green   Middlebere Heath   Wytch Heath   Newton Heath   Studland Bay   Freshwater Bay   Compton

ZONE   Grange Heath   East Creech   Norden   Isle of Purbeck   Studland   The Foreland or Handfast Point

Steeple   Church Knowle   Corfe Castle   Nine Barrow Down   Ballard Down   Ballard Point   Swanage Bay

Tyneham   Kimmeridge   Harman's Cross   Ulwell   Peveril Point

Broad Bench   SMEDMORE   Langton Matravers   Herston   Swanage   Durlston Bay

7   Worth Matravers   DURLSTON   Durlston Head   Tilly Whim Caves   Seacombe Cliff

St Aldhelm's or St Alban's Head   To Cherbourg

A   B   C   D   E

ENGLISH CHANNEL

0 1 2 3 4 5 10 15 kilometres
0 1 2 3 4 5 10 miles

**SURREY**

**WEST SUSSEX**

CAMBERLEY · Sandhurst · Yateley · Eversley Cross · Blackwater · FRIMLEY · Donkey Town · Chobham · West End · Bisley · Knaphill · WOKING · Horsell · Byfleet · West Byfleet · Wisley · Cobham · Stoke D'Abernon · Ashtead · EPSOM · BANSTEAD · Chipstead · Burgh Heath · LEATHERHEAD · Tadworth · Kingswood · Headley · Walton on the Hill

FLEET · Winchfield · Dogmersfield · Crookham Village · Church Crookham · FARNBOROUGH · North Town · Ash Vale · Normandy · Stoughton · Worplesdon · Send · Ripley · Ockham · Martyr's Green · Fetcham · Little Bookham · Great Bookham · Effingham · Mickleham · Box Hill · Pebble Coombe · Buckland

ALDERSHOT · Hale · Badshot Lea · Ash · Tongham · Wanborough · Onslow Village · GUILDFORD · Burpham · Merrow · West Clandon · East Clandon · West Horsley · East Horsley · West Humble · Betchworth · Brockham · REIGATE · DORKING · Wotton · Westcott · Gomshall · Shere · Albury · North Holmwood · South Holmwood · Leigh · Salfords

FARNHAM · Lower Bourne · The Bourne · Waverley · Charleshill · Shackleford · Peper Harow · Hurtmore · Compton · Loseley · Shalford · Chilworth · Blackheath · Albury Heath · Sutton · Friday Street · Abinger Common · Coldharbour · Parkgate · Norwood Hill · Horley · Hookwood

Bentley · Coldrey · Rowledge · Tilford · Elstead · Milford · Godalming · Busbridge · Bramley · Wonersh · Shamley Green · Farley Green · Peaslake · Holmbury St Mary · Beare Green · Newdigate · Charlwood · Gatwick (London)

Blacknest · Binsted · Wheatley · Kingsley · Bucks Horn Oak · Batt's Corner · Frensham · Rushmoor · Thursley · Wheelerstreet · Hydestile · Thorncombe Street · Grafham · Stroud Common · Rowly · Forest Green · Jayes Park · Ewhurst · Ockley · Capel · Rusper · Lambs Green · Ifield · County Oak · Fieldwood · CRAWLEY

Kingsley · Sleaford · Arford · Churt · Hindhead · Bowlhead Green · Wormley · Witley · Hambledon · Hascombe · Ewhurst · Walliswood · Oakwoodhill · Kingsfold · Faygate

Lindford · Headley · Grayshott · Grayswood · Brook · Loxhill · Dunsfold · Alford · Alford Crossways · Rudgwick · Ellen's Green · Rowhook · Warnham · Holmbush · Roffey · St Leonard's Forest · Colgate · Pease Pottage

Bordon · Whitehill · Blackmoor · Standford · Passfield · Bramshott · Shottermill · HASLEMERE · Camelsdale · Chiddingfold · Grayswood · Ramsnest Common · Fisherstreet · Ifold · Alfold · Loxwood · Rudgwick · HORSHAM · Broadbridge Heath · Mannings Heath · Handcross · Slaugham

Greatham · Liphook · Linchmere · Kingsley Green · Lythe Hill · Plaistow · The Haven · Buckman Corner · Five Oaks · Itchingfield · Barns Green · Broadbridge · Monk's Gate · Lower Beeding · Warninglid · Cuckfield

Langley · East Liss · Rake · Milland · Fernhurst · Blackdown Hill · Northchapel · Roundstreet Common · Newpound Common · Billingshurst · Southwater · Coneyhurst Common · Coolham · The Barn · Maplehurst · Crabtree · Cowfold · Bolney

Liss · West Harting · Hill Brow · Redford · Henley · Lickfold · Lurgashall · Balls Cross · Kirdford · Strood Green · Wisborough Green · Adversane · Broadford Bridge · Shipley · Dial Post · Partridge Green · Twineham · Hickstead

Rogate · Chithurst · Iping · Woolbeding · Lodsworth · Upperton · Gunter's Bridge · Burdocks · North Heath · Gay Street · West Chiltington · West Grinstead · Wineham · Sayers Common

Trotton · Nyewood · East Harting · Stedham · Easebourne · West Lavington · River Tillington · Petworth · Byworth · Egdean · Codmore Hill · Nutbourne · Thakeham · Ashington · Ashurst · Henfield · Albourne · Blackstone · Woodmancote

South Harting · Elsted · Treyford · Didling · Bepton · MIDHURST · Heyshott · Graffham · Selham · Duncton · Coates · Fittleworth · Stopham · PULBOROUGH · Hardham · Wiggonholt · Warminghurst · Bines Green · Oreham Common · Newtimber Place · Poynings

Uppark · North Marden · Cocking · Coultershaw Bridge · East Lavington · Barlavington · Watersfield · Sutton · Greatham · Rackham · Cootham · Storrington · Sullington · Washington · Wiston · Steyning · Bramber · Upper Beeding · Edburton · Fulking

Compton · East Marden · Chilgrove · Charlton · Upwaltham · Bignor · West Burton · Bury · Houghton · Amberley · North Stoke · Kithurst Hill · North End · Findon · Small Dole · Coombes

West Marden · Up Marden · Stoughton · Singleton · East Dean · West Dean · Slindon Estate · Goodwood · Madehurst · Dale Park · Eartham · South Stoke · Harrow Hill · Clapham · High Salvington · North Lancing · Kingston by Sea · Hangleton

Walderton · Woodend · Mid Lavant · East Lavant · Halnaker · Slindon · Arundel · Burpham · Wepham · Warningcamp · Patching · Salvington · North Lancing · South Lancing · SHOREHAM · Portslade-by-Sea · SOUTHWICK

Funtington · Westbourne · Westhampnett · Tangmere · Boxgrove · Norton · Walberton · Binsted · Cross Bush · Hammerpot · Durrington · Sompting · WORTHING · Shoreham-by-Sea · Portslade-by-Sea

Southbourne · Hambrook · Broadbridge · CHICHESTER · Oving · Aldingbourne · Westergate · Eastergate · Barnham · Ford · Yapton · Lyminster · Wick · Toddington · Rustington · East Preston · Angmering · Ferring · W. Tarring · Goring-by-Sea · West Worthing · Broadwater

Chidham · Fishbourne · Bosham · Apuldram · Donnington · Merston · Runcton · Colworth · Shripney · Burndell · Bilsham · Flansham · Climping · Littlehampton · Kingston by Sea · Poling

West Itchenor · Shipton Green · Birdham · Hunston · North Mundham · South Mundham · N. Bersted · S. Bersted · Middleton-on-Sea · Ancton · East Preston

Somerley · Highleigh · Street End · Sidlesham · Aldwick · Nyetimber · BOGNOR REGIS · Felpham

East Wittering · Earnley · Norton · Pagham · Church Norton · Selsey

Bracklesham Bay · Selsey Bill

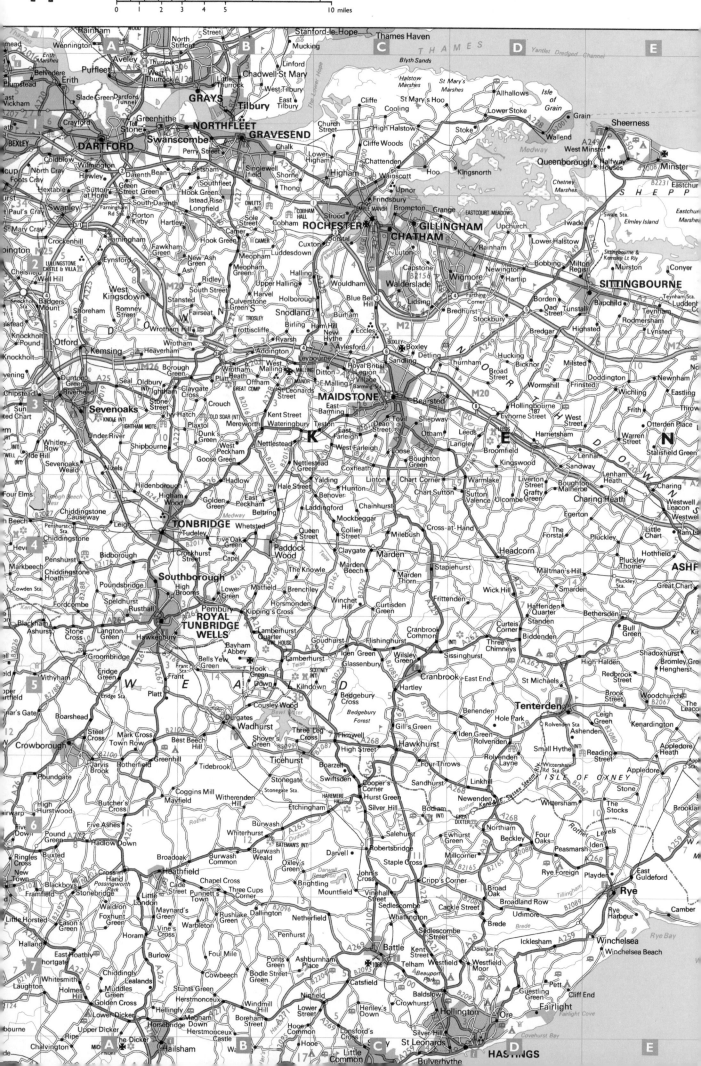

0 1 2 3 4 5     10        15 kilometres
0 1 2 3 4 5                10 miles

**A** **B** **C** **D** **E**

Brechfa · Pen-y-garn · Mynydd Figyn · Cwmdu · Llansadwrn · alfway · Dolgarreg · Y Pigwn · Llywel · Pentre'r · 417

Llanfynydd · Capel Isaac · Salem · Maerdy · Llangadog · Glan-Sefin · Myddfai · Mynydd Myddfai · Trecastell · Trecastle · Sennybridge · Defynnog · Penpont

325 317 · Plas · Pantglas Hall · Manordeilo · Felindre · Dyffryn Ceidrych · Rhiwiau Hill · Twynllanan · Llanddeusant · Usk Resr · Cefn Llechid

Felingwm · Court Henry · Broadoak · Llandeilo · Llangathen · Ffairfach · Bethlehem · Heol Senni

Pontargothi · Felindre · Dryslwyn · Maerdy · Capel Gwynfe · Pont-Aber · Cray · Fan Frynych 628 · Cnewr

Llanegwad · Golden Grove · Gelli Aur · Trapp · Truman · Pont Clydach · 802 · Moel Feity 591 · 603 · Beacon

Penrhiwgoch · Maesybont · Derwydd · Llandyfan · Black · Mountain · Foel Fraith 616 604 · Garreg-lwyd · Carreg-lem · Gareg-Goch · 562 · Cefn Cul · Fan-Gihirych 725 · Fan Fawr 734 · Fan Nedd · Fan Llia · Ystradfellte Resr

Porthyrhyd · Carmel · Pentre-Gwenlais · Tair Carn Isaf 459 · Bylchau Rhos-faen · Cefn Carn-Fadog · Cefn Mawr · Castell-y-geifr · Craig-y-nos · Penwyllt · Aber-Llia · Canc

Heol-ddu · Cefneithin · Gorslas · Llandybie · Brynamman · Cwmllynfell · Caer-Lan · CRAIG-Y-NOS · Carreg-lwyd · Bryn Bugeiliaid 382 · Aber-Craf · Coelbren · Pen-y-Cae · Ystradfellte

Drefach · Cross Hands · Tumble · Capel Hendre · Glanaman · Lower Brynamman · Gwaun-leision · Cwmgiedd · Abercraf · Caehopkin · Penderyn

Pontyberem · Saron · Penygroes · Betws · Garnant · Gwaun-Cae-Gurwen · Ystradgynlais · Penrhos · Onllwyn · Roman Road · Mynydd-y-glog

Llannon · Tycroes · Pantyffynnon · Cwmgors · Cwmtwrch-isaf · Gurnos · Coelbren · Pontbren Ilw

Pont Abraham · Ammanford · Pontamman · Tir-y-dail · Peullor-fedwen · Cwmllynfell · Dyffryn Cellwen · Mynydd-y-Drum · Mynydd y Gwair

Pont-henri · Graig Fawr · Mynydd Garn-fach · Egel · Cefn Gwrhyd · Ystalyfera · Varteg Hill · Seven Sisters · Pont Nedd Fechan · Penderyn

Mynydd Sylen · Fforest · Pentrebach · Cefn Drum 213 · Godre'r-graig · Allt-y-grug 339 · Glyn-Neath · Aber-pergwm · Morfa Glas · Blaengwrach · Cwmgwrach · Hirwaun

Sylen · Hendy · Pontardulais · Rhyd-y-fro · Langiwg · Swansea Valley · Hirfynydd · Aber-pergwm · Pont Walby · Rhigos · Penywaun

Horeb · Felinfoel · Craigcefnparc · Felindre · Pontardawe · Ynysmeudwy · Cilybebyll · Crynant · Pentreclwydau · Mynydd Resolfen 383 · Hirwaun Common · Cwmdare

Pwll · Llangennech · Dafen · Bolgoed · Trebranos · Alltwen · Rhos · Mynydd Machywel · Crynant · Rheola Forest · Cefn Grug · Craig-y-Llyn · Penywaun · DARE VALLEY

Llanelli · Bryn · Grovesend · Pontlliw · Vardre · Clydach · Glais · Bryn-coch · Resolven · Melincourt · Moel yr Hyrddod 493 · Blaenrhondda · ABERD

Elwynhendy · Bynea · Gorseinon · Ynystawe · Cilfrew · Cefn Mawr 536 · Cefntyle-brych · Tynewydd · Treherbert

Penllergaer · Llangyfelach · Morriston · Rhydding · Cadoxton-juxta-Tonna · Aberdulais · Glyncorrwg · Rho

Tir-deunaw · GLAMORGAN · WEST · Cwm · Pentre-dwr · Skewen · NEATH · Cefn Morfudd · Treorchy · 481

Loughor · Cadle · Birchgrove · Melincryddan · Cymmer · Blaengwynfi · Cwm-parc · Pentre

Pen-clawdd · Gowerton · Waunarlwydd · Llansamlet · Bon-y-maen · Pentre-chwyth · Pontrhyd-y-fen · Duffryn · Abergwynfi · Croeserw

Salthouse Pt · Crofty · Pound-ffald · Three Crosses · Dunvant · Cockett · Briton Ferry · Baglan · Pwll-y-glaw · Caerau · Mynydd Caerau · Wyrfa · Ton-Pentre

Llanmorlais · Cockett · Killay · Sketty · Kilvey Hill 193 · Foel Fynyddau 370 · Cwmafan · Bryn · Nant-y-moel · Llwynypia

Landimore · Llanrhidian · Oldwalls · Fairyhill · Ilston · Upper Killay · CLYNE VALLEY · Clyne · Aberavon · Mynydd Dinas 258 · Nantyffyllon · Pontycymer · PriceTown · Clydach Vale · Tonypandy

Cefn Bryn · W · Parkmill · Pennard · Common · Black Pill · West Cross · SWANSEA (ABERTAWE) · Port Talbot · Margam · Maesteg · Glan-llynfi · Garth · Blaengarw · Ogmore Vale · Wyndham · Peng

Knelston · Penmaen · Bishopston · Newton · The Mumbles · Taibach · Moel Margam · Llangynwyd 319 · Pont Rhyd-y-cyff · Ogmore Forest · Aber · GLAM

Oxwich · Penrice · Nicholaston · (NT) · Oxwich Bay · Mumbles Head · SWANSEA BAY · Moel Ton-mawr · Betws · Llangeinor · Blackmill · Glynogwr · Brynn

Oxwich Green · Oxwich Point · Pwlldu Head · Langland Bay · MARGAM PARK · Coytra-hen · BRYNGARW · Blackmill · Buarthfa · Mynydd y Gaer

Margam Burrows · Egln's Nunydd Resr · Mynydd Bryomenyn · Tondu · Bryncethin · Heol-y-Cyw

Kenfig Hill · Cefn Cribwr · Sarn · Aberkenfig · Common · Cefn Hirgoed · Bry

Kenfig Burrows · Mawdlam · Pyle · Cefn-Cross · Pen-y-fai · Pencoed · Tre-groe

Kenfig Pool · North Cornelly · Coity · M4 · Coychurch · St Mary

South Cornelly · Laleston · Newcastle · BRIDGEND · Craig Penllyn · Llansan · Llangan

Nottage · Tythegston · Treoes · Comtown · Wick · Llanmihangel · Sigingstone · Llanble

Porthcawl · Merthyr-mawr · Newton · Ogmore · Colwinston · Llandow

Porthcawl Pt · Ogmore-by-Sea · St Brides Major · Pitcot · Clemenstone · Nash

Tusker Rock · Southerndown · Ogmore-by-Sea · Llysworney · Broughton · Monknash

Marcross · St Donats · Llantwit Major · Boverto · G L

Nash Point

*B R I S T O L   C H A N N E L*

**A** **B** **C** **D** **E**

0 1 2 3 4 5 10 15 kilometres
0 1 2 3 4 5 10 miles

**A** **B** **C** **D** **E**

Aberfan
Merthyr Vale
Merthyr
Markham
Aberbeeg
Llanhilleth
Trevethin
branch
Glascoed
Usk
Llangwm
New Inn
Wolvesnewton
Kilgwrrwg Common
Devauden
Tintern Parva
Chapel Hill
Netherend
Brooke
Woolas

Bargoed
Oakdale
Argoed
Bargoed
Rock
Trinant
Crumlin
Penmaen
**PONTYPOOL**
Griffithstown
New Inn
Coed-y-paen
Llanllowel
Chepstow Park Wood
Newchurch
St Arvans
Boughspring
Woodcroft
Tutshill
Wibder

Gelligaer
Gilfach
Pengam
**Blackwood**
Mynydd Maen
Sebastopol
Pont-rhydyrun
Llanbadoc
Llangybi
Llantrisant
Gaerllwyd
Itton Common
Newland

Treharris
caiber
Trelewis
Penybryn
Fleur-de-Lis
Pontllanfraith
**Newbridge**
Upper Cwmbran
472
Pontnewydd
Groesyceiliog
Llandegveth
Pen-y-cae-mawr
Shirenewton
Mounton
**Chepstow**

Ystradmynach
Hengoed
Maesycwmmer
Cefn Hengoed
**Abercarn**
Cwmcarn
Pontywaun
Crosskeys
**CWMBRAN**
Henllys
Llanfrechfa
Tredunnock
Llanvair-Discoed
Pwllmeyric
Beachley
Mathern
Severn Road Bridge

Llanfabon
Cilfynydd
Mynydd Islwyn
Ynysddu
Wattsville
Castell-y-bwch
Llantarnam
Llanhennock
Komeys Inferior
Llanvaches
Penhow
Caerwent
Highmoor Hill
Crick
**CALDICOT CASTLE**
Oldbury Sands
Aust
Toll
Ingst

**Risca**
**Caerleon**
Malpas
Christchurch
Llanmartin
St Brides Netherwent
Caldicot
Rogiet
Portskewett
Sudbrook
Severn Beach
Northwick
Redwick
Awkle
Almon

Bedwas
Machen
Lower Machen
Rogerstone
**NEWPORT**
Milton
Underwood
Llanwern
Bishton
Wilcrick
Magor
Llanvihangel Rogiet
Undy
Summerleaze
DANGER ZONE
Severn Tunnel
Pilning
Easter Compton
Patchy

**CAERPHILLY**
Draethen
Rhiwderin
Bassaleg
Liswerry
**Steel Works**
Llandevenny
Redwick
Goldcliff
Whitson
Welsh Grounds
Caldicot Level
M5

Nantgarw
Glanyllyn
Thornhill
Castleton
Coedkernew
Marshfield
St Bride's Wentlooge
Pye Corner
Broadstreet Common
Nash

Rudry
PARC CEFN ONN
Cefn Mably
Begam
Michaelston-y-fedw
Blacktown

CASTELL COCH
Tongwynlais
Llanishen
Llanedeyrn
Pentwyn
St Mellions
Llanrumney
Peterstone Wentlooge

Whitchurch
Roath
Rumney

Llandaff North
Llandaff
Ely
Canton
**CARDIFF**

**MOUTH OF THE SEVERN**

Avonmouth
Battery Point
West Hill
Sheepway
Gordano
Shirehampton
Henbury

St Fagans
St Georges
Grangetown
Leckwith
Portbury
**Portishead**
Redcliff Bay
Pill
Easton-in-Gordano
Ham Green
Redland
Horfield

St Nicholas
Caerau
Michaelston-le-Pit
St Lythans
Wenvoe
Llandough
Cogan
**PENARTH**
Walton-in-Gordano
Weston-in-Gordano
Clapton-in-Gordano
Portbury
Failand
Leigh Woods
Abbots Leigh
Clifton
**BRISTOL**

St Andrews Major
Colcot
Cadoxton
Palmerstown
Dinas Powys
Lower Penarth
Cosmeston
Lavernock
Clevedon Court
Tickenham
Nailsea
Wraxall
Failand
Long Ashton
Barrow Gurney

Merthyr Dyfan
Sully
Lavernock Point
**Clevedon**
West End
Farleigh
Flax Bourton
Bishops

**BARRY**
Barry Island
Sully Island
St Mary's Grove
Kenn
Chelvey
West Town
Brockley
Downside
Upper Town
Felton
Dundry
Hill No Malre

Porthceri
Flat Holm
MIDDLE HOPE (NT)
WOODSPRING PRIORY
St Lawrence
Wick
Kingston Seymour
North End
Claverham
Cleeve
Lulsgate Bottom
North Wick
Chew Magna

Sand Point
Sand Bay
Kewstoke
Bourton
Yatton
Congresbury
Hewish
Puxton
East Rolstone
Redhill
Winford
Regil
Chew Stoke

Steep Holm
Toll
Milton
Worle
**WESTON-SUPER-MARE**
West Wick
Churchill
Wrington
Lower Langford
Butcombe
Nempnett Thrubwell
Chew Valley Lake

Weston Bay
Uphill
Locking
Hutton
Banwell
Sandford
Star
Burrington
Rickford
Blagdon
Ubley
West Harptree

Brean Down (NT)
Christon
Bleadon
Shiplate
Winscombe
Rowberrow
Black Down
Shipham
325
Charterhouse
Compton Martin
East Harptree

Brean
Bleadon Hill
Loxton
Cross
Lower Weare
Sidcot
KING JOHN'S HUNTING LODGE
Cheddar Cliffs
Cheddar Gorge
Mendip Forest

Berrow
Lympsham
Eastertown
Biddisham
Axbridge
**Cheddar**
CAVERNS
Cheddar Reservoir

BRIDGWATER BAY
Sedgemoor
Tarnock
Badgworth
Stone Allerton
Nyland Hill
Draycott
Priddy
Rodney Stoke

Gore Sand
Berrow Flats
Brent Knoll
East Brent
Rooks Bridge
Clewer
Westbury-sub-Mendip

Stert Island
**Burnham-on-Sea**
Edithmead
Chapel Allerton
Cocklake
Wookey Hole

Stert Flats
Mark Causeway
Mark
West Stoughton
Blackford
Wedmore
Easton
Wookey
**Wells**

Highbridge
Watchfield
Bason Bridge
Westham
Mudgley
Theale
Henton
Dinder

Huntspill
Cote
River Bridge
East Huntspill
Tadham Moor
Panborough
Yarley
Dulcote

Lilstock
Stolford
Steart
Stretcholt
Huntspill Level
Westhay Moor
Upper Godney
Polsham
Coxley

East Quantoxhead
Knighton
Burton
Shuton
Stockland Bristol
Pawlett
Blue
Westhay
Lower Godney
Meare
Worminster

Kilton
Kilve
Otterhampton
Down End
Catcott Burtle
Shapwick
Southway
Queen's Sedge Moor
North Wootton

atchet
St Audries
West Quantoxhead
Stringston
Holford
Dodington
Fiddington
Combwich
Puriton
Woolavington
Knowle Hall
Cossington
Edington
Catcott
**SOMER**
**Glastonbury**

Sampford Brett
Bicknoller
Nether Stowey
Over Stowey
Cannington
Chilton Trinity
Bawdrip
Chilton Polden
Stawell
Ashcott
Street
Glastonbury Tor 158
West Pennard

Stogumber
Crowcombe
Quantock Forest
Spaxton
Four Forks
Wembdon
Chedzoy
Shapwick
Walton
Overleigh
Edgarley
West Bradley
East Penna

**BRIDGWATER**

Willett
Flaxpool
Lower Aisholt
Enmore
Goathurst
Durleigh
**BRIDGWATER**
Westonzoyland
Moorlinch
Greinton
Pedwell
Compton Dundon
Baltonsborough
Ham Street

Combe Sydenham Hall
Lydeard St Lawrence
Tolland
West Bagborough
Merridge
Courtway
Broomfield
North Petherton
Northmoor Green or Moorland
Huntworth
Greylake
King's Sedge Moor
Henley
Dundon
Butleigh Wootton
Butleigh

Cothelstone
Combe Florey
Toulton
Cushuish
Goathurst
Durleigh Resr
Sedgemoor 1685
North Newton
Burrow Bridge
Othery
Aller
Low Ham
High Ham
Barton St David
Lydford W.

Ash Priors
Bishops Lydeard
Fulford
North Petherton
North Moorton
Stathe
Pathe
Bram
Charlton Mackrell
Keinton Mandeville

Langley Marsh
Fitzhead
Kingston St Mary
Combe Florey
Hedging
Lyng
Stathe
Aller
Low Ham
Bradley Hill
Littleton
Kingweston
Copley Wood
Charlton
Babcary

**A** **B** **C** **D** **E**

0 1 2 3 4 5    10    15 kilometres
0 1 2 3 4 5    10 miles

**A**    **B**    **C**    **D**    **E**    Tywyn

C A R D I G A N

**1**    Aberdy
Twy

B A Y    Uppe

**2**    Sarn Cynfelyn

Llangor
Cliff Rly
Aberystwyth
The Bar
Penparcau
Rhydyfelin
Llanfarian

**3**    Blaenplwy
Rhod-mad
Llanddeiniol

Carreg Ti-pw

Llanrhystud
Tref
Mabws
Rhydrosse
Llansantffraid    Llanon    Llyn f

**4**    Nebo
Aberarth    Cross Inn    Beth
Aberaeron    Penant
Monachty    Arth
Foss-y-ffin    Llanayron    Cilcennin
New Quay Head    New Quay    Llwyn-onn    Brynog    Bwlchllan
New Quay    bay    Llwynceilyn    Trefilan    B 43
Cwmtudu (NT)    Gilfachreheda    Ciliau-Aeron    Garth
Nanternis    Neuadd    Oakford    Talsarn    Abermeurig
Cross Inn    Llanarth    Dihewyd    Ystrad Aeron
Ynys-Lochtyn    Llwyndafydd    Mydroilyn    Temple Bar    13
(NT)    Synod Inn    Caledrhydiau    Bettws Bledr
**5**    Llangranog    Wervil    Plwmp    Cribyn    Silian
Pencribach    Brook    Capel St Silin
Aberporth    Penbryn    Pentregat    Talgarreg    Gors-goch    Aber
MWNT (NT)    Parcllyn    Tresaith    Brynhoffnant    Wstrws    Castell Howell    Cwrt-newydd    Lampeter
Cardigan Island    Sarnau    Capel Cynon    Cwmsychpant    Llanwnen
Cemaes Head    Gwbert-on-Sea    Tan-y-groes    Rhydlewis    Moel-y-mor    Pren-gwyn    12
Pen-yr-Afr    Verwig    Blaenannerch    Blaenporth    Glynarthen    Ffostrasol    Pontshaen    Rhydowen    Highmead
Pwllygranant    Penparc    Tremain    Bettws Evan    Hawen    Penrhiwpal    Tre-groes    Llanwenog    Drefach    Llanybyther
Tre-Rhys    Noyadd Trefawr    Brongest    Troedyraur    Maesllyn    Aber-banc    Penrhiwllan    Llanllwni    Abergiar    Pen
Cardigan    Pantgwyn    Beulah    Capel Dewi    258    Pencarreg    Tas-eithin
**6**    grove    St Dogmaels    Llangoedmor    Ponthirwaun    Horeb    Capel Dewi    Maescrugiau    415
Monington    Llechryd    Capel Tygwydd    Cwmcoy    Llandyfriog    Henllan    Pontwelly    Llanfihangel ar-Arth
Glanrhyd    Cilgerran    Manordeifi    Pont-Cen    Llanfair Orllwyn    Pentre-cwrt    383    408    Rhydcymerau
redrissi    Bridell    Cenarth    Pontwelly    Llandyssul    Llanllwni    368    326
y Hill    Trewilym    Llantood    Rhos Hill    PENTRE MANSION    Newcastle    Aberarad    Pentre-cagal    Drefach    Llangeler    Banc-y-ffordd
Nevern    Newchapel    Abercych    Emlyn    Henllan    Llidiadnenog
Velindre    Eglwyswrw    Penrherber    Pentre-cwrt
**D**    **Y**    **F**    **E**    **D**
Crosswell    Clyn-fiew    Velindre    Glynteg    Banc-y-ffordd
Brynberian    Llanfair    Boncath    Blaenffos    Penboyr    Bwlch-clawdd    257    Pencader    New Inn    Gwernogle
Tafarn-y-bwlch    Nant-Gwyn    Capel Iwan    Cwmpengraig    Rhos    Dol-gran    23    310
Ynydd Preseli    Whitechurch    Bwlch-y-groes    Glaspant    Gwyddgrug    Abergorlech
(Presely Mts)    Crymmych    Star    Clydey    Cwm Morgan    29    Alltwalis    355    Pen-y
Foel-cwmcerwyn    Hermon    Cilrhedyn    326    Gorllwyn    Cwmduad    Brechfa    Mynyd
536    Mynachlog-ddu    Foel-drych    Pentre-galar    Llanfyrnach    251    Hermon    Llanllawddog
Rosébush    **A**    368    **B**    Dinas    **C**    Esgair    **D**    Pontarsais    **E**
Maenclochog    Glandwr    Hebron    Trelech    Llanpumsaint

0 1 2 3 4 5    10    15 kilometres

0 1   2   3   4   5    10 miles

**W A R W I C K**

**O X F O**

REDDITCH

Henley-in-Arden

ROYAL LEAMINGTON SPA

Warwick

Southam

Napton on the Hill

Studley

Astwood Bank

Alcester

Stratford-upon-Avon

BANBURY

Evesham

Shipston on Stour

Chipping Campden

Broadway

Moreton-in-Marsh

Winchcombe

Stow-on-the-Wold

Chipping Norton

Charlbury

Woodstock

BLENHEIM PALACE

Bourton-on-the-Water

Burford

Witney

Northleach

Carterton

Bampton

Cirencester

Lechlade

Fairford

**36**

0 1 2 3 4 5    10    15 kilometres
0 1 2 3 4 5    10 miles

**A**    **B**    **C**    **D**    **E**

Llangollen   Newbridge   Erbistock   Horseman's Green   Lightwood Green   Penley   Eglwys Cross   **Whitchurch**   Edgeley

Moel Fferna 630   Pentre   Shellbrook   Knolton   Trench   Park Lane   Hanmer   The Chequer   Alkington   Tilstock

Plas Nantyr   Pontfadog   Halton   Street Dinas   Sodylt Bank   Gredington   Arowry   Bronington   Platt Lane   Prees Higher H

Glyn Ceiriog   Dolywern   Chirk   Rhyn   Ifton Heath   Higher Grange   Welshampton   Bettisfield   Hollinwood   Prees

Pen-plaenau 541   Bryn Du 563   Pandy   Bronygarth   Preesgweene   Gledrid   Dudleston Heath   Welsh End   Whixall

Cadair Bronwen 784   Foel Wen   Llwynmawr   St Martin's   Weston Rhyn   New Marton   Ellesmere   Northwood   Quina Brook   Prees Green

Tregeiriog   Llechrydau   Craignant   Rhewl   Gobowen   Perthy   COLEMERE   Lyneal   Paddolgreen   Edstaston

Llanarmon Dyffryn Ceiriog   Selattyn   Hengoed   Hindford   Welsh Frankton   Colemere   Newtown   Wolverley   Prees Green Sta

Garneddwen 496   Brogyntyn   **Whittington**   Babbinswood   Kenwick   English Frankton   Loppington   Tilley   **Wem**   Aston   Brockhurst

Rhiwlas   Rhydycroesau   Llawnt   Middleton   Rednal   Lower Hordley   Cockshutt   Noneley   Bury Walls   Hopto

Llanrhaeadr-ym-Mochnant   Trefonen   Ball-Maesbury Marsh   Queen's Head   Haughton   Grimpo   Bagley   Petton   Burlton   Aston   Besford

**Oswestry**   Morda   West Felton   The Cross   Eardiston   Weston Lullingfields   Myddlewood   Alderton   Clive   Preston Brockhurst

Pentrefelin   Treflach   Morton   Woolston   Weirbrook   Wykey   Stanwardine in the Fields   Baschurch   Myddle   Yorton   Grinshill   Moreton Corbet

Llangedwyn   Nantmawr   Llynclys   Knockin   Dovaston   Ruyton-XI-Towns   Prescott   Milford   Walford   Oldswood   Harmer Hill   **Shawbury**   Hadnall

**Llanfyllin**   Porth-y-waen   Maesbrook   Kinnerley   Crosslanes   Kinton   Little Ness   Nesscliffe   Grafton   Bomere Heath   Preston Gubbals   Astley

Llanfechain   Llanymynech   Llandysilio   Edgerley   Wilcott   Great Ness   Felton Butler   Albrighton   Haughton   Poynton Green

Llanfihangel   Godor   Four Crosses   Domgay   Melverley Green   Pentre   Leaton   Fitz   Poynton   Roden   Walt

Deuddwr   Waen-Fach   Sarnau   Llandrinio   Melverley   Ensdon   The Isle   Forton   Montford   Uffington

Tycwryn   Trefnanney   Ardd-lin   Crew Green   Alberbury   Shrawardine   Montford Bridge   Bicton   Battlefield   Rodington

Meifod   Pentrebeirdd   Geufford   Criggion   Breidden Hill 365   Middletown Hill   Wollaston   Ford   Montford   Bicton Heath   Shelton   **SHREWSBURY**   Upton Magna   Walco

Pontrobert   Guilsfield   Pool Quay   Moel-y-Golfa   Middletown   Ivyend   Cardeston   Shoot Hill   Nox   Meole Brace   Norton

Heniarth   Groesllwyd   Trewern   Garreg Bank   Halfway House   Yockleton   Cruckton   Bayston Hill   Sutton   Atcham   Wroxeter

**Welshpool (Y Trallwng)**   Buttington   Stretton Heath   Westbury   Stoney Stretton   Cruckmeole   Lea   Great Hanwood   Hook-a-Gate   Cross Houses   Donni

Llanfair Caereinion   Castle Caereinion   Hope   Vennington   Lower Wallop   Farley   Edge   Hinton   Annscroft   Great Lyth   Berrington   Dryton

Llwynderw   Fron   Short Cross   Rowley   Westley   Asterley   Pontesford   Plealey   Longden   Condover   Cantlop   Upper Cound   Cound   Cressa

Pant-y-ffridd   Leighton   Trelystan   Brockton   Leigh   Minsterley   Worthen   Ploxgreen   Habberley   Wrentall   Church Pulverbatch   Dorrington   Great Ryton   Golding

Manafon   Aberriw (Berriew)   Forden   Kingswood   Marton   Binweston   Hope   Snailbeach   Pulverbatch   Acton Burnell   Acton Pigott   Broomcroft

New Mills   Vaynor Park   Garthmyl   Wotherton   Betton   Meadowtown   Rorrington   Gravels   Perkins Beach   Cothercott   Longnor   Frodesley   Ruckley   Kenley

Tregynon   Brooks   Chirbury   Black Marsh   Middleton   Pennerley   Shelve   Picklescott   Woolstaston   Leebotwood   Church Preen   Hughley   Westwo

Bettws Cedewain   Priestweston   Corndon Hill 513   The Bog   Bridges   Ratlinghope   Caer Caradoc   Cardington   Enchmarsh   Plaish   Bour

Abermule   Landyssil   **Montgomery (Trefaldwyn)**   Cefn-y-coed   Church Stoke   Hyssington   Black Rhadley Hill   All Stretton   Caer Bowdler   **Church Stretton**   Gretton   Longville in the Dale   Easthope   WILDERHOPE MANOR   Shipton

Llanmerewig   Pentreheyling   Snead   Norbury   Wentnor   Linley   Little Stretton   East Wall   Wall Bank   Rushbury   Shipton Hall

**Newtown (Y Drenewydd)**   Llanllwchaiarn   Sarn   Lydham   More   Asterton   Myndtown   Hope Bowdler   Wall under Heywood   Ticklerton   Eaton   Stan

Kerry   Glan-Mule   **Bishop's Castle**   Lea   Eaton   Minton   Marshbrook   Acton Scott   Harton   Alcaston   Broadstone   Middlehope   Holdgate

Cefn-gwyn   Mainstone   Colebatch   Plowden   Eyton   Whittingslow   Woolston   Whitton   Munslow   Westhope   Tugford

Dolfor   Kerry Hill   Edenhope Hill   Cefn-Einion   Brockton   Lydbury North   Horderley   Edgton   Wistanstow   Dinchope   Corfton   Diddlebury   Peaton   Upper He

Clun Forest   Anchor   Hall of the Forest   Offa's Dyke   Acton   Bryn   Lower Down   Walcot   Cheney Longville   Sibdon Carwood   Halford   Siefton   Great Sutton   Weston   Stoke St Mill

Cilfaesty Hill 528   Black Mountain   Whitcott Keysett   Bicton   Kempton   Hopesay   Aston on Clun   Craven Arms   Culmington   Vernolds Common   Lower Hayton   Upper Hayton   Hayton's Bent   Hopton Cangeford

Bryn Gydfa   Felindre   Newcastle   Bettws-y-crwyn   Llwyn   Little Brampton   Clunton   Purslow   Clunbury   Broome   Onibury   Stokesay   Norton

Moel Wilym 469   Beguildy   Quabbs   **Clun**   Woodside   Black Hill 441   Clunbury Hill   Twitchen   Hopton Castle   Clungunford   Stanton Lacy   Middleton   Bitterley

Llanbadarn Fynydd   Dutlas   Llanfair Waterdine   Llanfair Hill   Hurgin   Hobarris   Obley   Bedstone   Wootton   Shelderton   **Ludlow**   Bromfield

Gorslydan   Moelfre Hill   Beacon Hill 547   Purlogue   New Invention   Hopton Titterhill   Henley   Caynham Camp   Ludford   Caynham

Brynmelyn   Lloyney   Five Turnings   Chapel Lawn   Stow Hill   Leintwardine   Kinton   Bringewood Chase   Downton on the Rock   Snitton   Titter Clee

Llanbister   Knucklas   Stowe   Bucknell   Buckton   Brampton Bryan   Walford   Burrington   Aston   Henley   Overton   Bleddfa   Hob Bag

**Knighton**   Bailey Hill   Panpunton   Milebrook   Adforton   Elton   Leinthall Starkes   Richard's Castle   Ashford Bowdler   Ashford Carbonel   Wooffert

Glog Hill   Pilleth   Wigmore   Newton   Letton   Leinthall Starkes   Hereford

**A**    **B**    **C**    **D**    **E**

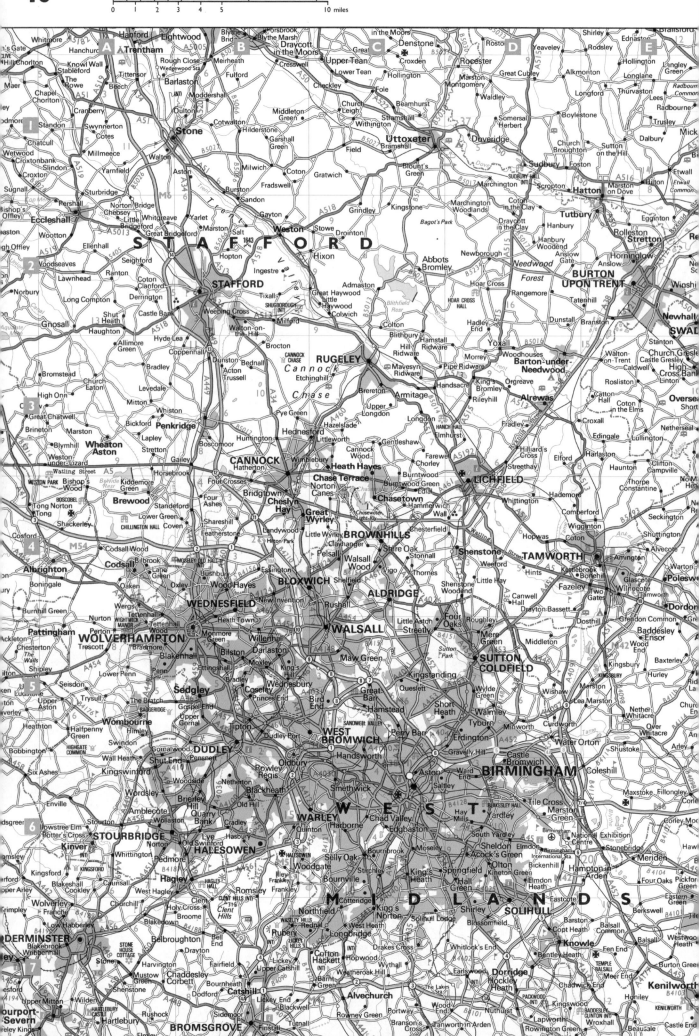

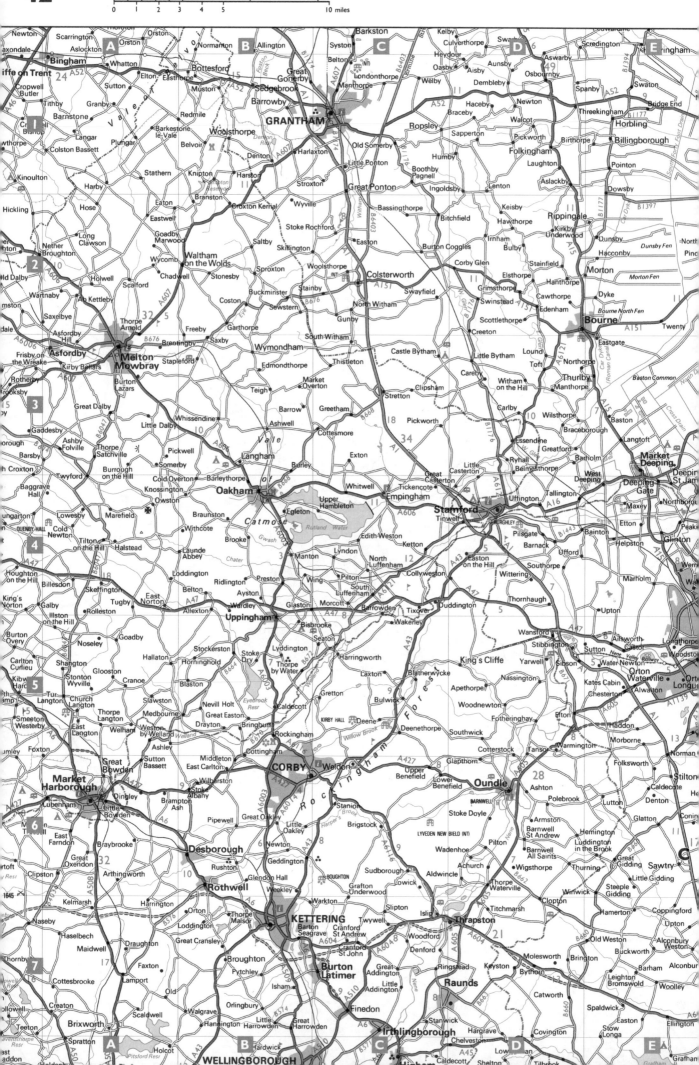

0 1 2 3 4 5 10 15 kilometres
0 1 2 3 4 5 10 miles

**A   B   C   D   E**

**I**

**2**

**3**

**4**

**5**

**6**

**7**

**8**

The Skerries
West Mouse
Cemaes Bay
Llanbadrig
Porth Wen Bay
Bull Bay
Point Lynas
Carmel Head
Neuadd
Burwen
Amlwch
Llaneilian
Pengorffwysfa
Tregele
Cemaes
Llanfairynghornwy
Llanfechell
Bodewryd
Rhosgoch
Penysarn
Dulas
Ynys Dulas
Llanrhyddlad
Carreglefn
Llanflewyn
Parys Mountain
Rhydwyn
Llanfairynghornwy
Llanfaethlu
Llanbabo
Llanddeusant
Ceidio
Llanerchymedd
City Dulas
Rhosybol
Brynrefail
Moelfre
Ligwy Bay
Church Bay
Llanfwrog
A5025
Alaw
Carmel
Llanfigael
Pen-llyn
Llyn Llywenan
Llechcynfarwy
Llandyfrydog
Brynteg
Llanallgo
Marian-glas
HOLYHEAD
Llanfachraeth
Bodffordd
A5
Maenaddwyn
Benllech
North Stack
Holyhead Mountain 220
Llanynghenedl
Bodedern
Capel Coch
Red Wharf Bay
Holyhead (Caergybi)
Salt Island
A N G L E S E Y
Llanbedrgoch
Red Wharf Bay
South Stack
Llaingoch
Kingsland
Penrhos
Valley
Caergeiliog
Trefor
Llangwyllog
Tregaian
Llanddyfnan
Mynydd Llwydiarth
Penrhyn Mawr
Trearddur Bay
Four Mile Bridge
Bryngwran
Llynfaes
Rhosmeirch
Pentraeth
B5109
HOLY ISLAND
Rhoscolyn
Bodior
Llanfair-yn-Neubwll
Capel Gwyn
Gwalchmai
Cerrigceinwen
Heneglwys
Llangefni
Penmynydd
Llansadwrn
Llandegfan
Rhosneigr
Tywyn Trewan
Llanfaelog
Tycroes Sta.
B4422
Llangristiolus
Pentre Berw
Penmynydd
Ceint
B5420
Garth
Menai Bridge
Bethel
Trefdraeth
Gaerwen
Llanddaniel Fab
Llanfairpwllgwyngyll
Aberffraw
Llangadwaladr
Hermon
Malltraeth
Llangaffo
Brynsiencyn
Port Dinorwic
Seion
Bodorgan
Malltraeth Sands
A4080
Dwyran
Waen-wen
Tal-
Newborough (Niwbwrch)
B4419
Waterloo Port
Bethel
Penisar Waun
Llanddeiniolen
Malltraeth Bay
Newborough Warren
Pont-rug
Llanrug
Llanddwyn Island
Caernarfon
Bryn Bras
Caeathro
Cwm-y-glo
Llanberis
Llanddwyn Bay
Abermenai Point
The Bar
Llanfaglan
A487
Llanwnda
Dinas
Bontnewydd
Betws Garmon
Moel Eilio 726
Salem
C A E R N A R F O N
Llandwrog
Rhostryfan
Rhosgadfan
Carmel
Moel Tryfan
Mynydd Mawr 698
B A Y
Glynllifon Park
Groeslon
Nantlle
Talysarn
Y Garn 634
Penygroes
B4418
Llyn Nantlle Uchaf
Pontllyfni
Trwyn Maen Dylan
Llanllyfni
Nebo
Nasareth
Garneddgoch 700
Clynnog-fawr
Tai'r-lôn 221
Capeluchaf
Pant-glas
Beddgelert
Trwyn y Gorlech
Yr Eifl 564
Trevor
Gurn Ddu
Moel Hebog 782
Bwlch Mawr 509
Upper Clynnog
Pen-sarn
Cennin
Bryncir
Moel-d
Llyn Cwmystradllyn
Pistyll
Llithfaen
Llanaelhaearn
Cefn-caer-Ferch
Rhoslan
Garn Dolbenmaen
Dolbenmaen
Golan
Morfa Nefyn
Nefyn
Llwyndyrys
Llangybi
Prenteg
Moel-y-Gest
Tremadog
Groesffordd
Garn Boduan
Edern
Fron
Fourcrosses
Llanarmon
Gell
Penmorfa
Pentrefelin
Porthmadog
Rhôs-y-llan
Ceidio Fawr
Bodfuan
Chwilog
Llanystumdwy
Criccieth
Morfa Bychan
Tudweiliog
Dinas
Llannor
Abererch
Pen-ychain
Black Rock Sands
Traeth Bach
Carn Fadryn
Efailnewydd
A497
Garn 371
Rhyd-y-clafdy
Pwllheli
Harlech Point
Llanfihangel-y-traethau
Aber
Llaniestyn
Penrhyn Mawr
Sarn-Meyllteyrn
Rhedyn
Penrhos
Carreg yr Imbill
Tý-hen
Botwnnog
Nanhoron
Y Gamlas
Morfa Harlech
Methlem
Rhydlios
Bryncroes
Llandegwning
Mynytho
Llanbedrog
Trwyn Llanbedrog
Harlech
Capel Carmel
Llidiardau
Llawr-y-dref
Mynydd Rhiw 305
Llangian
Morfa Dyffryn
Braich Anelog
Mynydd Anelog 191
Bwlch-y-Rhiw
Rhydolion
Abersoch
St Tudwal's Road
Llandanwg
Pwlldefaid
Aberdaron
Llanfaelrhys
Sarn-bâch
Llanengan
Bwlchtocyn
St. Tudwal's Islands
Llanbedr
Braich y Pwll
Uwchmynydd
Aberdaron Bay
Ynys Gwylan-fawr
Cilan Uchaf
Porth Neigwl or Hell's Mouth
Llanddwywe
Pen y Cil
Bardsey Sound
Porth Ceiriad
Trwyn yr Wylfa
Trwyn Cilan
Dyffryn Sta.

TREMADOG BAY

To Dublin & Dun Laoghaire

0 1 2 3 4 5 10 15 kilometres
0 1 2 3 4 5 10 miles

A B C D E

To Belfast

To Douglas

Mad Wharf
Formby Hills (NT)
Freshfield
Formby Point
Formby

Barton
Haskayne
Downholland Cross
Great Altcar
ORMSKIRK
Halsall
Aughton Park
Town Green
Scarth Hill
Westhead
Newburgh
SKELMERSDALE
BEACON PARK
Roby Mill
Up Holland
Dalton
Appley Bridge
Appley Br. Sta.
Shevington Moor
Shevington
Standish
WIGAN
Gathurst

Hightown
Ince Blundell
Little Crosby
Thornton
Netherton
Sefton
Lunt
MAGHULL
Melling Mount
Aughton
Bickerstaffe
Crawford
Barrow Nook
Rainford
Crank
Billinge
Garswood
Bryn
Moss Bank

CROSBY
Great Crosby
Waterloo
Seaforth
LITHERLAND
Ford
Melling
Aintree
KIRKBY
Kirkby Industrial Estate
Knowsley
ST HELENS
Eccleston
Earlestown
Haydock
West Park
Thatto Heath
Collins Green
New

BOOTLE
New Brighton
Walton on the Hill
CROXTETH HALL
LIVERPOOL
West Derby
Knotty Ash
Roby
Prescot
Rainhill
Whiston
Sutton Leach
Burtonwood

WALLASEY
Seacombe
Bidston
Moreton
Upton
MERSEYSIDE
Childwall
Huyton
Rainhill Stoops
Cronton
Bold Heath
Great Sankey
Penketh

Hoylake
East Hoyle Bank
West Hoyle Bank
Hilbre Island
Massie
Saughall
Greasby
BIRKENHEAD
Woodchurch
Prenton
Rock Ferry
Mossley Hill
Woolton
Gateacre
Halewood
Hough Green
Farnworth
Ditton

West Kirby
Point of Ayr
Talacre
Caldy
Grange
Frankby
Irby
Barnston
Pensby
New Ferry
Aigburth
Grassendale
Allerton
Hunt's Cross
WIDNES
Moore

Thurstaston
THE WIRRAL
Heswall
Gayton
BEBINGTON
Port Sunlight
Garston
Speke
RUNCORN
Weston Point
Weston
Halton
Frodsham

River Dee
Dawpool Bank
Brimstage
Bromborough
Eastham
Eastham Sands
Dungeon Banks
Ince Banks
Norton
Preston Brook
Sutton Weaver
Aston

Danger Zone
White Sands
Parkgate
Neston
Little Neston
Ness
Burton
Puddington
Shotwick
Childer Thornton
Hooton
Stanlow Point
Mount Manisty
ELLESMERE PORT
Whitby
Elton
Helsby
Hapsford
Alvanley
Newton
Kingsley
Crowton
Norley

Gronant
Gwespyr
Ffynnongroyw
Mostyn Bank
Holywell Bank
Bagillt Bank
Parkgate

Llanasa
Trelawnyd
Mostyn
Glan-y-don
Llannerch-y-môr
Greenfield
Willaston
Overpool
Great Sutton
Ledsham
Little Stanney
Thornton-le-Moors
Stoak
Dunham on-the-Hill
Manley
Hatchmere
Delamere

Downing
Whitford
Lloc
Carmel
Walwen
HOLYWELL
Bagillt
Capenhurst
Backford
Wervin
Picton
Bridge Trafford
Mickle Trafford
Guilden Sutton
Ashton
Mouldsworth
Kelsall
Delamere Sta.
Eddisbury Hill

FLINT
Flint Mountain
Northop Hall
Shotton
Mancot
Saughall
Mollington
Upton
Hoole
Littleton
Tarvin
Oscroft
Willington Corner
Cotebrook
Quarrybank
Duddon

Connah's Quay
Garden City
Queensferry
Sealand
Blacon
CHESTER
Christleton
Guilden Sutton
Rowton
Burton
Clotton
TARPORLEY
Tilstone Fearnall

Mold
Buckley
Ewloe
Aston
Sandycroft
Hawarden
Broughton
Saltney
Handbridge
Eccleston
Saighton
Huxley
Birch Heath
Tiverton
Alpraham

Padeswood
Penyffordd
Lower Kinnerton
Dodleston
Cuckoo's Nest
Eaton Hall
Hatton Heath
Gatesheath
Hargrave
Tattenhall
Beeston
Bunbury

Hope
Caergwrle
Burton Green
Pulford
Lavister
Rossett
Trevalyn
Aldford
Churton
Handley
Coddington
Milton Green
Newton
Tattenhall
Burwardsley
Spurstow

Ruthin
Llanbedr-Dyffryn-Clwyd
Llanfwrog
Bwlchgwyn
Cefn-y-bedd
Llay
Marford
Gresford
Holt
Farndon
Clutton
Chowley
Harthill
Broxton
Bickerton
Peckforton
Peckforton Hills
Haughton
Bulkeley

WREXHAM
Gwersyllt
Moss
Southsea
Rhosddu
Rhosnesni
Wrexham Industrial Estate
Ridleywood
Tilston
Duckington
Egerton Green
Bickley Town
Bickley Moss
Malpas
No Man's Heath
Norbury
Chorley

Bersham
Rhostyllen
ERDDIG
Marchwiel
Pentre Maelor
Shocklach
Bowling Bank
Worthenbury
Threapwood
Tallarn Green
Wirswall
Whitchurch

Rhosllanerchrugog
Johnstown
Stryt-yr-hwch
Bangor-is-y-Coed
Oldcastle Heath
Cuddington Heath
Marley Green
Wrenbury

Penycae
Acrefair
Ruabon
Eyton
BANGOR-ON-DEE
Royton
Overton
Penley
Eglwys Cross
Edgeley

Cefn Mawr
Newbridge
Erbistock
Lightwood Green
Horseman's Green
The Chequer

Llangollen
Valle Crucis
Llantysilio
Trevor
Froncysyllte
Pentre
Halton
Shellbrook Hill

Corwen
Glyndyfrdwy
Moel Ferna 630
Pontfadog
Glyn Ceiriog
CHIRK CASTLE (NT)
Chirk
Street Dinas
Arowry
Bronington
Alkington

Horseshoe Pass
World's End 492
Llantysilio Mountain
Moel y Gamelin 577
Bryneglwys
Llandegla
Coedpoeth
Minera
Esclusham Mountain
Rhos Berse
New Broughton

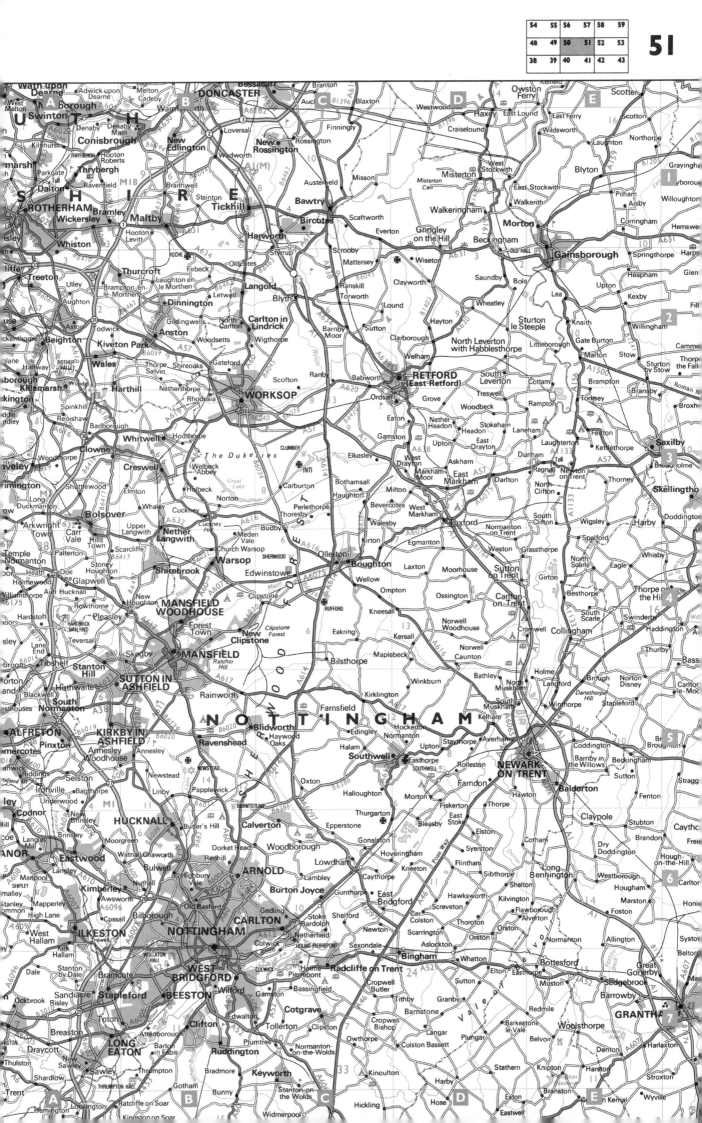

0 1 2 3 4 5    10    15 kilometres
0 1 2 3 4 5    10 miles

A    B    C    D    E

BARROW-IN-FURNESS
North Scale    Dendron    Aldingham    Capernwray    Gressingham
Newbarns    Gleaston    Over Kelle    Hornby
Vickerstown    Roosecote    Leece    Newbiggin    Carnforth    Nether Kellet
    Rampside    Bolton-le-Sands    Moorgate    Claugh
Tummer Hill Scar    MORECAMBE    Slyne    Halton    Caton
Biggar    Hest Bank    Brookhouse
WALNEY ISLAND    Roa Island    Cartmel    Wharf    Caton M
Mort Bank    West End    Torrisholme    Crossgill
South End    Sheep Island    Foulney Island    Yeoman Wharf    Sandylands    Blanch Fell
    Piel Island    Oxcliffe Hill    LANCASTER    Quernmore    Ward
Hilpsford Point    Piel Bar    HEYSHAM    Heaton    Scotforth    Clougha Pike
    Middleton    Stodday    Lee Fell
To Douglas    Overton    Conder Green    Tarn
    Sunderland Bank    Glasson    Greenbank    Lee
    Sunderland Point    Lower Thurnham    Galgate    Abbeyste
    Upper Thurnham    THURNHAM HALL    Dolphinholme    Wyre
    Cockerham    Forton    Street    Hawthornth Fell 479
    Braides    Forton
    Bernard Wharf    Winmarleigh    Scorton    Calder
    Knott End-on-Sea    Fisher's Row    Oakenclough
North Wharf    Pilling Lane    Pilling    Stake Pool    Calder Vale
Rossall Point    PILLING    Garstang    Park
FLEETWOOD    Preesall    Bowgreave    Brock
    Stalmine    Eagland Hill    Nateby    Claughton
Cleveleys    Staynall    Churchtown    Catterall    White Chapel
Burn Naze    Trunnah    Hambleton    Ratten Row    BEACONF
Little Bispham    Thornton    Mosside    St. Michael's on Wyre    Bilsborrow    Inglewhite
Norbreck    Hambleton    Out Rawcliffe    Great Eccleston    LANC
Bispham    Whin Lane End    Toll    Elswick    Cuddy Hill    Goosnargh
Poulton-le-Fylde    Singleton    Crossmoor    Inskip    Barton    M6
North Shore    Normoss    Thistleton    Roseacre    Newsham    Haighton Green
BLACKPOOL    Staining    Esprick    Greenhalgh    Wharles    Gatforth
Great Marton    Weeton    Swillbrook    Woodplumpton    Broughton
    Great Plumpton    Wesham    Treales    Cottam    Sharoe Green
South Shore    M55    Kirkham    Salwick Sta.    1648    Fulwood
Squires Gate    Common Edge    Westby    Lea Town    Ribbleto
    Blackpool    Higher Ballam    Wrea Green    Clifton    Fishwick
St. Anne's    Moss Side    Freckleton    Penwortham    PRESTON
LYTHAM ST ANNE'S    Ansdell    Saltcotes    Warton    Hutton    Walton-le-Dale
Salter's Bank    Lytham    RIBBLE    Longton    New Longton    Bamber Bridge
    Banks Sands    Walmer Bridge    Midge Hall    Tardy Gate    CUERDEN VALLEY
    Hesketh Bank    Much Hoole    Farington
    Becconsall    Leyland    Clayton-le-Woods
Horse Bank    Hundred End    Whittle-le-Woods
    Banks    Tarleton    Bretherton    ASTLEY HALL
Angry Brow    Marshside    Sollom    Croston    Euxton
    Churchtown    Mere Brow    Eccleston
SOUTHPORT    Holmeswood    Rufford    Charnock Richard
    Birkdale    RUFFORD OLD HALL (NT)    Heskin Green    Coppul
    Brown Edge    Tarlscough    Mawdesley    Charnock Richard
    Snape Green    New Lane Sta.    Wrightington Bar    Coppul Moor
Mad Wharf    Shirdley Hill    Bescar    Burscough    Hoscar Sta.    Parbold    Shevington Moor
    Scarisbrick    New Lane    Burscough Bridge    Appley Bridge    Standish
Ainsdale    Pinfold    Burscough    Newburgh    Appley Bri.    Shevington
    Halsall    Dalton
    Barton    Westhead    BEACON PARK
Formby Hills    Haskayne    ORMSKIRK    Roby Mill    Gathurst
Formby Point    Freshfield    Downholland Cross    Aughton Park    Scarth Hill
Formby    Great Altcar    SKELMERSDALE    WIGAN
    Town Green    Up Holland    ORRELL
    Aughton    Bickerstaffe    Crawford    Bryn
Hightown    Ince Blundell    Maghull    Barrow Nook    Garswood
Little Crosby    Lunt    Melling Mount    Rainford    Billinge
    Thornton    Sefton    Kirkby Ind. Est.    Crank    Moss Bank
CROSBY    Netherton    Melling    KIRKBY
Waterloo    Great Crosby    Ford    Aintree
LITHERLAND    Kirkby

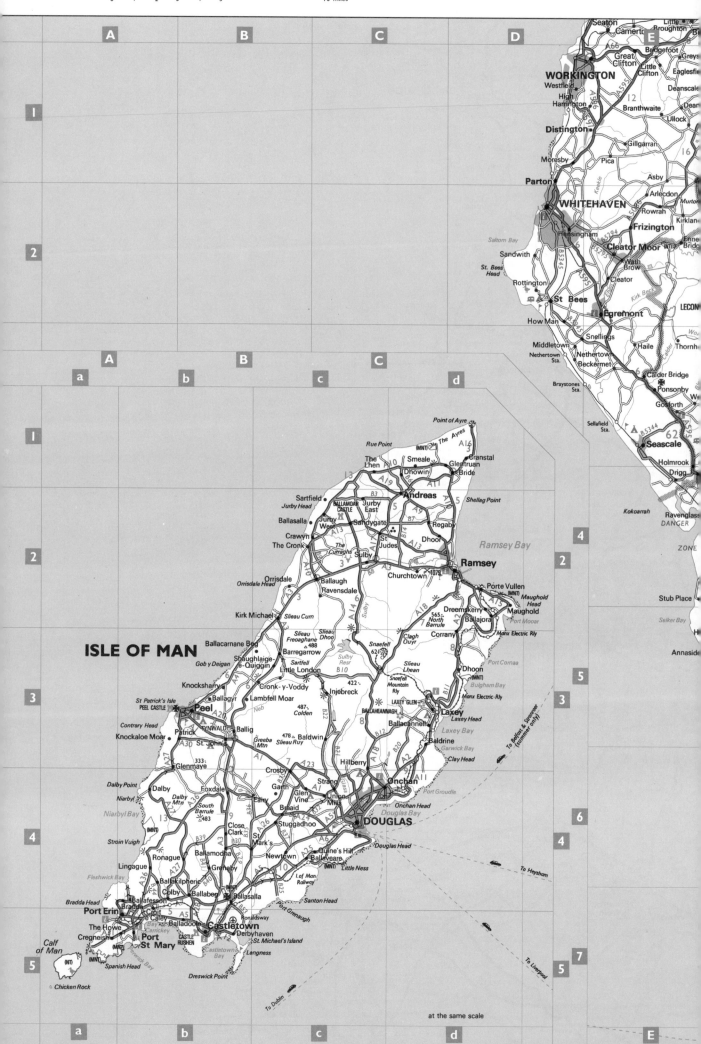

0 1 2 3 4 5    10     15 kilometres
0 1 2 3 4 5    10 miles

**ISLE OF MAN**

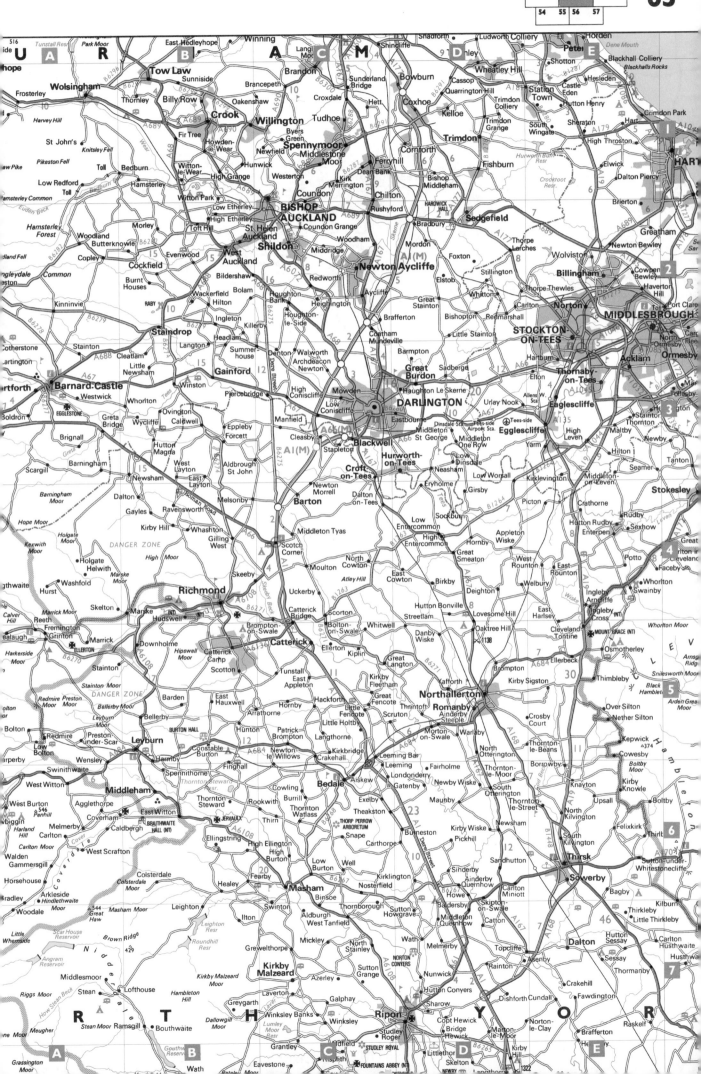

0 1 2 3 4 5    10    15 kilometres

0 1 2 3 4 5    10 miles

A    B    C    D    E

**1**

Ailsa Craig

Chapeldonan   Trochrague   Ba   Dailly

B741   Deil's Elbow

Old Daily   Hadyard Hill   Garleffin Fell 429   Linfern Loch

**Girvan**   Penkill

Saugh Hill   Penwhapple Reservoir

Glendoune   Glengennet   North Balloch

Black Neuk   Glendrissaig   South Balloch

Ardwell   Pinminnoch

Kennedy's Pass   Grey Hill 297   **Barr**

C   Changue Forest

Lendalfoot   Pinmore   B734 A R R

13   Water of Lendal

Aldons   Polmaddie Hill 565

Carleton Fishery   Daljarrock   Loch Scalloch

Bennane Head   Poundland   Pinwherry   · 479   Sha

**Colmonell**   Shalloch Well   GA

**2**

Dalreoch   Glenduisk   Muck Water   Kirmeeroch Loch   F

A765   Craigneil   Black Clauchrie   Loch Moan

Ballantrae Bay   Knockdolian   Ballochmorrie

Mains of Tig   **Barrhill**   Garwall Hill

B7044   Water of Tig   Loch Goosey

**Ballantrae**   Auchairne   Balkissock   Shiel Hill   Eldrick   A714   **30**

Low Kilphin   Lochton   Corwar House

Glenapp Castle   High Kilphin   22

Downan Point   **30**   Drumlamford Loch   **Glencaird**

Kilantringan Loch   Craigie Fell   Beneraird 339   Chirmorie   Drumlamford   Bargrennan

Carlock Hill   Milljoan Hill   Loch Dornal

**3**

To Lorne   Finnarts Point   Altimeg Hill   Benbrake Hill   Loch Maberry   Clauchaneasy

Milleur Point   Markdow   Larg

Corsewall Point   Glen App   Miltonise   Loch Ochiltree   Polnaskie

Barnhills   Glenwhilly   Knockville

North Cairn   17   Urrall Fell   Knowe

Dunan Bay   South Cairn   Corsewall   Cairn Point   Dalnigap   Black Burn   G B7027

**Kirkcolm**   Cairnryan   Loch Ree   Main Water of Luce   Glenrazie   L

Airies   Ervie   Artfield Fell   Carseriggan   Challoch

Portobello   St Mary's Croft   Braid Fell   Balminnoch   **Newton S**

**4**

Slouchnawen Bay   Knocknain   Leswalt   Soleburn Bridge   Culvennan Fell   Shennanton   Benf

B7043   **New Luce**   T H E   M O O R S

Lochnaw Castle   Innermessan   Auchmantle   Loch Ronald   **Kirkcowan**

A718   Lochinch Castle   Black Loch   Craig Fell   Galdenoch   Barlae   Craighlaw

CASTLE KENNEDY   15   Baraer

Broadsea Bay   **Stranraer**   Loch Magillie   Carscreugh   A75

Portslogan   A75   Castle Kennedy   Dunragit Moor   25   Dernaglar Loch   Spittal

Whiteleys   Soulseat Loch   10   Whitecairn   Knock Moss   Clugston Loch

**5**

Black Head   Lochans   **Dunragit**   Whitefield Loch   Knock Fell   Castle Loch   **Corsemalzie**

Dinvin   Cairn Pat   Kildrochet   Genoch   Whitecrook   **Glenluce**   Mochrum Loch   Barnbar

**Portpatrick**   A77   8   Colfin   Genoch Square   A757   A75   Crows Nest   Culshabben

DUNSKEY CASTLE   Awhirk   **Stoneykirk**   10   Sands of Luce   Auchenmalg   Alticry   Elng Loch   **Loch Head**

Port of Spittal Bay   Balgreggan   G   35   B7005   Elrig

Cairngarroch Bay   **Sandhead**   Auchenmalg Bay   Longcastle   Airyhassan

**6**

Money Head   Awhirk   9   L U C E   B A Y   Mochrum   A714

Ardwell Bay   Ardwell   Barr Point

Drumbreddan Bay   Chapel Rossan   DANGER ZONE   **Port William**   White Loch   M

Logan   Portacree

**Mull of Logan**   New England Bay   Barsalloch Point   Monreith

Port Logan   Terally   Monreith Bay   Cre

Kilstay   Cairndoon

**7**

Clanyard Bay   **Drummore**

Laggantalluch Head   Kirkmaiden   Cailliness Point   St Nini

Crammag Head   Damnaglaur   Scares

Dunman   Maryport   Portankil

Nick of Kindram

West Tarbert   East Tarbert

To Douglas (summer only)   **Mull of Galloway**

A    B    C    D    E

**DUMFRIES & GALLOWAY**

Loch Bradan Reservoir, Loch Muck, Loch Finlas, Waterhead, Craiglee, Starr, Loch Head, Loch Riecawr, Shiel Hill, Benbrack, Bow Burn, Cairnsmore of Carsphairn, Dodd Hill, Colt Hill, Countam, Auchenbrack, Torbraehead, Auchenhessnane, DRUMLANRIG, Holm, Carronbridge, Dabton, Morton Loch

Drumjohn, Lamloch, Brochloch, Coran of Portmark, Garryhorn, Knockgray, Craig of Knockgray, Black Shoulder, Bail Hill, Benbuie, Bennan, Eccles, Thornhill, Burnhead, Penpont, Gatelawbridge

Carsphairn, Bardennoch, Marscalloch Hill, Cornharrow Hill, Carroch, Wether Hill, Clonrae, Tynron, Keir Mill, Keir Hills, Closeburn, Croalchapel

Rinns of Kells, Corserine 813, Meaul 695, Dalshangan, Castlemaddy, Forrest Lodge, Polmaddy Burn, Carstad Loch, Moniaive, Crawfordton, Kirkland, Craigdarroch, Glencrosh, MAXWELTON, Crossford, Barndennoch, Blackwood, Glenhead

Carlin's Cairn, Millfire 716, Burnhead, Knocknalling, Knockgray, Corriedoo, Castlefairn, Holmhead, Lochurr, Bogrie Hill 432, Sundaywell, Milton, Dunscore

Merrick 843, Loch Enoch, Craignaw, Buchan Hill, Loch Neldricken, Loch Valley, Loch Dungeon, Earlstoun Loch, Bogue, Waterhead, Loch Skae, Craigenputtock, Stroquhan, Speddoch, Newtonairds, Gribton

Mulldonoch, Lamachan Hill 716, Larg Hill, Garroch, Glenlee, St John's Town of Dairy, Holm, Balmaclellan, Blackcraig, Scroggie Hall, Knocklearn, Gibbshill, Garcrogo Forest, Corsock, Slongaber, Magreig, Skeoch Hill, Glenkiln Resr, Scaur

Craignelder, Cairnsmore of Fleet 711, New Galloway, Kenmure Castle, Clatteringshaws, Cairnsmore of Dee, Larglear Hill, Corsock Loch, Glen 398, Shawhead, Henderland, Brae, Lochfoot

Millfore, Craigencallie, Darnaw, Round Fell, Fell of Fleet, Shaw Hill 471, Bennan Toll, Drumrash, Glenlair, Merkland, Square Point, Kirkpatrick Durham, Springholm, Crofts, Brooklands, Crocketford or Ninemile Bar, Milton, Beeswing, Lotus Hill

Door of Cairnsmore, Auchencloy Hill, Airie Hill, Slogane, Mossdale, Hensol, Shieldhill, Barwhillanty, Loch Roan, Auchendolly, Old Bridge of Urr, Hermitage, Stonehouse, Kirkgunzeon

Minnigaff, Cumloden, Blackcraig, Dallash, Bargaly, Cairnsmore, Craig, Palnure, Spittal, Barholm, Creetown, Cassencarie, Glenquicken Moor, Cairnharrow 456, Castramont, Ruskoo, Barlay, Lauchentyre, Loch Whinyeon, Glengap, Ringford, Barcaple, Argrennan, Airieland, Netherthird, Tongland Loch, Screel Hill 391, Bengairn, Kippford or Scaur, Colvend, Rockcliffe, Port o' Warren, Castlehill Point, Almorness Point

Laurieston, Glenlochar, Hillowton, THREAVE CASTLE, Castle Douglas, Dalbeattie, Craig Nair, Dalbeattie Forest, Barnbarroch, Fairgirth

Little Duchrae, Craig, Valleyfield, Tongland, Cumstoun, Bridge of Dee, Buchan, Rhonehouse or Kelton Hill, Breoch, Gelston, Palnackie

Gatehouse of Fleet, Anwoth, Ardwall, Girthon, Barwhinnock, Twynholm, Barharrow, Sandgreen, Langlands, High Borgue, Lennox Plunton, Knockbrex, Borgue, Kirkandrews, Senwick, Ross, Barclay, Barcloy, Bombie, Bankhead, Hazelfield, Auchnabony, Rascarrel, Dundrennan, Orroland, Balmae

Wigtown, Wigtown Sands, Baldoon Sands, Carsluith, Kirkdale, Cardoness, Fleet Bay, Murray's Isles, Islands of Fleet, Ardwall Island, Barlocco I., Wigtown Bay, Kirkcudbright, St Mary's Isle, Townhead, Abbey Head, Little Ross, Ringdoo Point, Boreess, Cruggleton Bay

Kirkinner, Stewarton, Eggerness, Sorbie, Cults, Garlieston, Innerwell Port, Orchardton Bay, Whithorn, Portyerrock, Kidsdale, Cutcloy, The Devil's Bridge, Isle of Whithorn, Burrow Head, Port Allen

DANGER ZONE, Port Mary, Balcary Point, Hestan Island, Auchencairn Bay, Rascarrel Bay, Barlocco Bay

Roads: A713, A762, A702, A712, A75, A745, A711, A746, A714, A747, A710, B729, B7000, B7009, B795, B727, B796, B794, B797, B7052, B7063

0 1 2 3 4 5      10      15 kilometres
0 1 2 3 4 5        10 miles

**D U M F R I E S**

**& G A L L O W A Y**

A   B   C   D   E

Moniaive   Crawfordton   Kirkland   Keir Hills   Croalchapel   Blackacre   Dinwoodie Mains   Bore
Craigdad   Glencrosh   Maxwelton   Crossford   Barndennoch   Dalswinton Common   Ae Village   Wester Parkgate   Shawfoot   Hangingshaw   Corsehill
Wether Hill   Castlefairn   Bogrie Hill 432   Sundaywell   Blackwood   Glenhead   Nethermill   Cumrue   Templand   Sibbaldbie   Gillenbie   Her
Holmhead   Lochurr   Milton   Dunscore   Crawston Hill   Allanton   Dalswinton   Glenae   Duncow   Millhousebridge
Corriefeoo   Waterhead   Loch Skae   Loch Urr   Stroquhan   Friars Carse   Amisfield Town   Lochmaben   Lockerbie   Tund
Loch Howie   Craigenputtock   Speddoch   Gribton   Kirkton   Tinwald   Heck   Hightae   ROMAN CAMP
Blackcraig Hill   Drumwhirn   Newtonairds   Holywood   New Bridge   Locharbriggs   Castlemilk   Kettleholm
Scroggie Hall   Knocklearn   Slongaber   Magreig   Skeoch Hill   Terregles   LINCLUDEN   Torthorwald   RAMMERSCALES   Ecclefecha
Gibbshill   Garcrogo Forest   Scaur   DUMFRIES   Noblehill   Collin   Carthat Hill   Dalton
Larglear Hill   Corsock   Glen 398   Shawhead   Cargenbridge   Racks   Cleuchbrae   Carrutherstown
Corsock Loch   Merkland   Crofts   Henderland   Brae   Lochfoot   Goldielea   Kingholm Quay   Woodside   Mouswald
Drumrash   Glenlair   Square Point   Brooklands   Crocketford or Ninemile Bar   Dalskairth   Cargen   Netherwood   Bankend
Shieldhill   Walton Park   Kirkpatrick Durham   Springholm   Milton   Mabie   Kelton   Lochar Moss   Longbridge Moor   Clarencefield   COMLONGON
Parton   Barwhillanty   Gillfoot   Loch Arthur   Whinny Hill   Glencaple   Shearington   Ruthwell   KINMOUNT   Ann
Little Duchrae   Auchendolly   Old Bridge of Urr   Stonehouse   Beeswing   Lochaber Loch   Kirkconnell   Shambellie   SWEETHEART   CAERLAVEROCK   Blackshaw   Cummertrees   Powfoot
Craig   Crossmichael   Hermitage   Kirkgunzeon   Kinharvie   New Abbey
Loch Ken   Clarebrand   Molance   Haugh of Urr   Lotus Hill   Loch Kindar   Merse
Launeston   Glenlochar   Townhead of Greenlaw   Hillowton   Cuil Hill   Blackshaw Bank   Bown
THREAVE CASTLE   Castle Douglas   Dalbeattie   569 Criffell   Carse Bay
Bridge of Dee   Buchan   THREAVE   Rhonehouse or Kelton Hill   Breoch   Gelston   Craig Nair   Dalbeattie Forest   Kirkbean   Cavens   Cardurnoc
Ringford   Dildawn   Argrennan   Palnackie   Barnbarroch   Caulkerbush   Borron Point   Grune Point
Barcaple   Netherthird   Airieland   Fairgirth   Mainsriddle   ARBIGLAND   Skinburness   Newton A
Valleyfield   Screel Hill 391 Bengairn   Kippford or Scaur   Douglas Hall   Preston Merse   Southerness   Silloth   Calvo   Seaville
Tongland   Cumstoun   Rockcliffe   Colvend   Port o' Warren   Mersehead Sands   Southerness Point   Blitterlees   Causewayhead   Abbeytown
Kirkcudbright   Barcloy   Castlehill Point   Barnhourie Sands   Beckfoot   Pelutho   Highlaws   Blencog
Bombie   Bankhead   Auchencairn   Almorness Point   Mawbray   Aikshaw   Bromfield
Auchnabony   Hazelfield   Hestan Island   Dubmill Point   Edderside   Langrigg
St Mary's Isle   Rascarrel   Balcary Point   Allonby   Westnewton
Townhead   Dundrennan   Orroland   Rascarrel Bay   Hayton   Aspatria   Blennerhass
DANGER ZONE   Balcarro Bay   Allonby Bay   Crosscanonby   Allerby   Arkleby   Plumbland
Abbey Head   Port Mary   S O L W A Y   Crosby   Gilcrux   Parsonby
Maryport   Ellenborough   Dearham   Moota Hill   Sunderland   Blindcrake
Flimby   Broughton Moor   Doveny   Tallentire   Bridekirk   Great Broughton
Seaton   Camerton   Little Broughton   Brigham   Cockermouth   Embleton   WORDSWORTH HOUSE
WORKINGTON   Great Clifton   Little Clifton   Bridgefoot   Greysouthen   Eaglesfield   Thornthwa Forest
Westfield   High Harrington   Branthwaite   Dean   Deanscales   Ullock   Pardshaw   High Lorton
Distington   Gillgarran   Mockerkin
Moresby   Pica   Asby   Lamplugh   Loweswater   Brackenthwaite Fell
Parton   Cogra Moss   Loweswater Fell
WHITEHAVEN   Murton Fell   Crummock

0 1 2 3 4 5 10 15 kilometres
0 1 2 3 4 5 10 miles

**A** **B** **C** **D** **E**

Hope House
Clintburn
Chirdon Burn
Hetherington
Birtley
Sweethope Loughs
Great Bavington
Capheaton
Whalton
Saltwick
Spy Rigg
Round Top
Stonehaugh
Wark
Colt Crag Resr
Thockrington
B6342
Belsay
Ogle
Black Heddon
Westgate
Higham Dykes

**I** Whygate
Park End
Chipchase Castle
Great Swinburne
Kirkheaton
Kearsley Fell
Ryal
Ingoe
Milbourne
Ponteland
13
Wark Forest
Sheperdshield
Nunwick
Simonburn
Gunnerton
Barrasford
Colwell
Hallington
Hallington Resr
Matfen
Stamfordham
Hawkwell
Dalton
Ouston
Darras Hall
High Callerton
Lampert
Black Fell
Hadrian's Wall Vallum
Haughton Common
Humshaugh
Walwick
Chollerton
Bingfield
Grindstonelaw
Fenwick
Heugh
Horsley
Wylam
Callerton Lane End
Black Callerton

**2** Whiteside
Greenlee Lough
Broomlee Lough
VERCOVICIVM (HOUSESTEADS) (NT)
Crag Lough
Hadrian's Wall Vallum
B6318
Fourstones
Newbrough
Warden
Low Brunton
Wall
Hadrian's Wall Vallum
Stagshaw Bank
Halton
Great Whittington
Little Whittington
B6321
Aydon
Newton
Harlow Hill
Rudchester
Heddon on the Wall
Throckley
NEWBURN
Lemington
Hadrian's Wall Vallum
VINDOLANDA
Stanegate
Bardon Mill
56
Henshaw
Haydon Bridge
A69
Low Gate
Hexham
TYNE GREEN
Corbridge
Sandhoe
Ovington
Ovingham
Crawcrook
Ryton
Stella
BLAYDON
Haltwhistle
A69
Melkridge
Willimontswick
Acomb
Sunnyside
Dilston
Stocksfield
Mickley Square
Prudhoe
Greenside
Plenmeller (NT)
Unthank Hall
Plenmeller Common
B6305
Newbiggin
Linnels
Riding Mill
Broomhaugh
Painshawfield
Coalburns
High Spen
Barlow

**3** Rowfoot
Lambley
Stonehouse
Asholme Common
Fellhouse Fell
Whitfield Bearsbridge
Whitfield Moor
Stublick
Catton
West Dipton Burn
Dalton
Dotland
Whitley Chapel
Slaley
Healey
Hedley on the Hill
Leadgate
Highfield
Row Gill
Chopwell
Whittonstall
Hamsterley
Lintzford
Hobson
Newlands
Burnopfield
Whitfield
South Tyne
B6303
Allendale Town
Studdon
Hexhamshire Common
Broadwell House
Devil's Water
Slaley Forest
Barleyhill
Kiln Pit Hill
Shotleyfield
Ebchester
Medomsley
Dipton
STANLEY
A686
Ninebanks
Sinderhope
Hangman Hill
Blanchland Moor
Pow Hill
Derwent Resr
Buffside
Carterway Heads
Shotley Bridge
DERWENT WALK
Mugglewick
Consett
Leadgate
Annfield

**4** Whitfield Law
Kirkhaugh
Axle
Mohope Moor
Hartley Moor
Spartylea
Green Hill
Hope Fell
Allendale Common
Blanchland
Edmundbyers
Hunstanworth
Nookton Fell
Cross Rigg
Mugglewick Common
Smiddy Shaw Resr
Healeyfield
Allensford
Castleside
Delves
Iveston
Healey
Rowley
Knitsley
Greencroft Hall
Lanchester
S. Tynedale Rly
B6294
Coalcleugh
Allenheads
561
Redburn Common
Bolt's Law
Waskerley Resr
Waskerley
Butsfield
Cornsay
Satley
Cornsay Colliery
Waterhouses
East Hedleyhope
Alston
A689
Middle Fell
Nenthall
Killhope Moor
Stangend Currick
B6295
Rookhope Burn
Rookhope
Stanhope Common
Skaylock Hill 516
Grawleyside
Wolsingham Park Moor
Tunstall Resr

**5** Garrigill
Nenthead
Cornriggs
Cowshill
Wearhead
Middlehope Moor
675
Newbiggin Common
Stanhope
Frosterley
Harvey Hill
St John's
Knitsley Fell
Pikeston Fell
Low Redford
Toll
Bedburn
Hamsterley
Tow Law
Sunniside
Thornley
Billy Row
Fir Tree
Howden-le-Wear
Witton-le-Wear
Crook
Rotherhope Fell
Round Hill
Burnhope Reservoir
Ireshopeburn
St John's Chapel
Daddry Shield
Westgate
Eastgate
A689
Hill End
Bollihope Common
Pawlaw Pike
Hamsterley Common
Woodland
Morley
Toft Hill
Witton Park
Low Etherley
High Etherley
Milburn Forest
Bellbeaver Rigg
Burnhope Seat
Viewing Hill
Harwood
Ireshope Moor
Three Pikes
Chapel Fell
Chapelfell Top 696
Westernhope Moor
Snowhope Hill
Outberry Plain
Middleton Common
Carrs Hill
Woodland Fell
Hamsterley Forest
Langleydale Common
Copley
Evenwood
Butterknowle
B6282
West Auckland

**6** Cross Fell
Knock Fell
Langdon Beck
Forest
Widdybank Fell
Cow Green Resr
Caldron Snout
Cronkley Fell
Newbiggin
Holwick
Monks Moor
High Force
Eggleston
Woodland
B6281
Cockfield
Burnt Houses
Wackerfield
Hilton
Raby
10
Ingleton
Dufton
Keisley
Backstone Edge
High Cup Nick
Murton Fell
Mickle Fell 790
Lune Forest
Middleton in Teesdale
Lune Moor
Bowbank
Mickleton
Eggleston
Kinninvie
Staindrop
Hutton Magna
Murton
Hilton
DANGER
Hilton Fell 745
Burton Fell
ZONE
Fish Lake
Iron Band 562
Thringarth
B6276
Grassholme
Grassholme Resr
Romaldkirk
Hunderthwaite
Cotherstone
Stainton
Lartington
A688
Cleatlam
Langton
Brackenber
Coupland
Warcop
Hillbeck
Stainmore Common
North Stainmore
47
Beldoo Hill
Hunderthwaite Moor
Baldersdale
Balderhead Resr
Clove Lodge
Cotherstone Moor
Deep Dale
Startforth
Barnard Castle
Westwick
Whorlton
Ovington
Caldwell

**7** Nettle Hill
Smardale
Waitby
Kirkby Stephen
Great Asby
Bleatarn
Great Musgrave
Brough
Little Musgrave
Brough Sowerby
Kaber
Argill Beck
13
Bowes Moor
Bowes
Gilmonby
A66
Brignall
Barningham
Newsham
West Layton
Crosby Garrett
Winton
Soulby
Hartley
Winton Fell
Kaber Fell
Sleightholme Moor
Stainmore Forest
Scargill
Scargill High Moor
Dalton
Ravensworth

**A** **B** **C** **D** **E**

72

0 1 2 3 4 5    10    15 kilometres
0 1 2 3 4 5    10 miles

A    B    C    S T R    D A    T    E    H

Point of Knap

**A**

*'w-landman's Bay*
*ron Garbh*
*Bhride*
*' lean Leanachais*

Loch Chaorunn
Dubh Chreag
Meall Reamhar    480
Stonefield    Barmore Island
Barfad    East Loch Tarbert
Craignafeich    Auchenlochan
Derybruich    Kames
Millhouse
Portavadie    Glenmore    Kames Hill    Stuck
Strone Point    Ardr

Drum...shaig
Larach na Gaibhre
Cretshengan
Coulaghailtro
Kilberry Head
Kilberry
Keppoch Point
Cruach Airde
Dunmore

Stottfield Bay
Miller's Bay
Loch nan Torrar
Meall Reamhar
Loch a Chaoruinn
Loch Racadal
Port Ban

Dubhchladach
Tarbert
West Tarbert
Escart
Corranbuie
Achadacaie
Kennacraig
Cruach an t'Sorchain
Cruach Doire Leithe
421
Cnoc a Bhaile-shios
Redhouse
Whitehouse
Coire nan Capull
Gartnagrenach
Gartavaich
Glenrisdell
Skipness
Skipness Point
Culindrach
Altagalvash

Low Stillaig    Kilbride
Blair's Ferry
Carry    Glecknabae
Drumachloy    Kilbride    Bannatyne
Ardlamont    Upper Ardroscadale    Port
Rubha Lagganroaig    Ardlamont Point    Meikle Kilmory    Rothesa
Camas na Ceardaich    Ardi...

Port Leatham
Mealdarroch Point
Asgog Bay    Kilbride Bay
Ardiamont Bay    Blindman's Bay    Ettrick Bay
Scalpsie Bay

*Inchmarnock*
St Ninian's Point
Midpark
Ardscalpsie
*SOUND OF BUTE*
Dunagoil Bay    Garro...
Stravanan Bay    Garro...

**1**

Carse
Ardpatrick
Rubha Cruitiridh
Achadh-chaorrunn

Portachoillan
Quinhill
Clachan
52

To Askaig
West Tarbert Bay
To Port Ellen
West Tarbert Bay    East Tarbert Bay
Tarbert
Ardaily
Port Mor
Drumyeon Bay

Loch Stornoway

Cruach nam Fiadh    269
Claonaig
Rockfield
Escair
North    Crossaig
South

(summer only)
Loch Ranza
Cock of Arran
North    Newton
South

**2**
*SOUND OF BUTE*
Stravanan    Kil...
Port Fada

**Gigha Island**
Arminish
Craro Island
Arminish Bay
*SOUND OF GIGHA*
Cruach Mhic-Gougain
North South
Loch Garasdale
Loch Ciaran
Escairt
Talatoll
Corrchrevie
**Ballochroy**
Auchinafaud

Grob Bagh
Cara Island
**Mull of Cara**
Cleit Dhubh
A Chleit

Rhunahaorine Point
Rhunahaorine
Narachan Hill    285
Cnoc-an t'Samhlaidh
Cnoc Reamhar
Cout    21
Cour Bay
Rubha Airigh Bheirg
Craw
Lenimore
Mid Thundergay    Beinn Bhreac
South Thundergay    711    573
Pirnmill    Beinn Tarsuinn
Beinn Bhreac
721
Beinn Bharrain

Catacol Bay
Glen Catacol
Lochranza
Glen Chalmadale
North Glen Sannox    14
Glen Sannox
Sannox Bay
Mid Sannox
Caisteal Abhail
Cir Mhor    798
Cioch-na-h-Oighe
Goat Fell    874
Corrie

**3**
Tayinloan
**Killean**
Beacharr
Achaglass
Cruach nan Gabhar    354

Diollaid Mhor
Deucheran Hill
Sunadale
Grogport
Carradale Water

*KILBRANNAN SOUND*
Whitefarland Point
Imachar
Balliekine
Glen Iorsa
Iorsa Water
Beinn Tarsuinn    825
Beinn Nuis
Glen Rosa    (NTS)
**ARRAN**
Merkland Point
BRODICK CASTLE
*Brodick Bay*

**4**
Muasdale
Arinanuan    426
Belloch
Glenbarr
Beinn Bhreac
Rhonadale
Dippen
Carradale
Torrisdale
Beinn an Tuirc    436
Whitestone

Glenacardoch Point
Barr Water
Carradale Bay

Dougarie Point
Dougarie
An Tunna
Water
Glaister
Machrie
Tarrnacraig
A'Chruach
Ard Bhainn    512
Beinn Bhreac    503
Ballymichael

Machrie Bay
11
Benlister Glen
Glencloy
**Brodick**
Strathwhillan
Corriegills
5
Margnaheglish
Lamlash
Glenkiln
Holy Is...
Lamlash Bay

**5**
N
374    Meall Buidhe
**Saddell**
Bunlarie
Corrylach
Killocraw
Sgreadan Hill    397    13
Ballochgair
Skeroblingarry
Glen Lussa
Drumgarve
Callyburn
Peninver
Tangy

Lussa Loch
Tangy Loch
Port Crom
Saddell Bay
Ugadale Point
Ardnacross Bay

Torbeg
Shiskine
Blackwaterfoot
Kilpatrick
Brown Head
Drumadoon Bay
Glen Scorodale
Tormore

Kingscross
Knockenkelly
Kiscadale
Whiting Bay    458
Ashdale
Largymore
Largybeg    Largybeg Poin...
Dippin    Dippin Head
*Whiting B...*

**6**
Westport
Ballivain
Kilchenzie
East Darlochan
Kilmichael
Drumore
Campbeltown
Machrihanish
Drumlemble
Dalivaddy
Witchburn
Campbeltown Loch
Davaar I.
Davaar

Machrihanish Bay

Drumlemble
Chiscan
Oatfield
Killypole
Kilchrist
Killellan
385    The Slate
Knocknaha
Glenramskill
Beinn Ghuilean
Kilkerran
B843
New Orleans
352
Chiscan Water
Arinarach Hill

Corriecravie
Sliddery
Lagg    20    A841
Shannochie
Bennan Head
Kildonan
*Pladda Sound*
*Pladda*

Cnoc Moy    446    Largybaan
Cnoc Reamhar
Conie Water
Cnoc Odhar    276
Brecklate
Glen Breackerie
Beinn na Lice
428
Garveld
Feorlan

Feochaig
Sheanachie
Ru Stafnish
Drum Kilavie
Keprigan
Macharioch
Keil
Southend
Polliwilline Bay

**7**
*Mull of Kintyre*
Borgadelmore Point
Carskey Bay

*Sanda Sound*
Sheep Island

**Sanda Island**

*Ailsa C...*

A    B    C    D    E

0 1 2 3 4 5     10     15 kilometres
0 1 2 3 4 5     10 miles

**A**   **B**   **C**   **D**   **E**

Lochcraig Resr
Ballageich Hill △330
Polnoon
Auldhouse
Currochfauld
CALDERGLEN
rland
Rutherend
Quarter
Limekilnburn
Fairholm
han
all
Law
Dalserf
Carluke
Netherto
B7056

Kingswells
Corsehouse Resr
Bennan Loch
Dunwan Dam
Melowther Hill
Lochgoin Reservoir
Chapelton
Glassford
Udstonhead
Rosebank
Netherburn
Milton Lockhart
Kilcadzow
Harelaw
Carstairs
Carn

Waterside
Lochgoyn
375 △ Laird's Seat
Ardochrig
Strathaven
Netherfield
Stonehouse
Draffan
Braidwood
Crossford
Nemphlar
Jerviswood
Lanark
Ravensruther
Carstairs Junction
Libb

Ardochrig
Calderill
Hairshaw
Sandford
Blackwood
Kirkmuirhill
Boghead
Auchenheath
Hazelbank
Kirkfieldbank
New Lanark
Hyndford Bridge
Pettinain
Cairngryffe Hill
Covington

Pley Moss
Cauldcoats
Kype Muir
Lesmahagow
Birkwood
Auchlochan
Hawksland
Bonnin
Linn
Cairngryffe Hill

Newmilns
Darvel
Greenholm
Galston
Priestland
1307
Dungavel
Auchingilloch
Goodbush Hill
Nutberry Hill 522
Coalburn
Braehead
Bankend
Rigside
Uddington
Stone Hill
Thankerton
St John's Kirk
Tinto 707
Symir

Milrig
Middleyard
Changue Hill
Auchmannoch Muir
Distinkhorn
Wedder Hill
Mill Rig
Glengavel Reservoir
Priesthill Height
Logan Water
Robert Law
Scaur Hill
Wiston
Dungavel 510
Roberton

Mossgiel
Blairkip
Mid Hill 430
Dun Rig
Middlefield Law
Black Hill
Glenbuck
Hazelside
Glespin
Douglas
Redshaw
Wildshaw Hill

Nethershield
Nether Wellwood
Boghead
Greenock Water
Muirkirk
Kames
Parishholm
Glenbuck

Catrine
Gilmilnscroft
Airds Moss
Cronberry
1680
Carbellow
Cairn Table 593
Dryrigs Hill
Crawfordjohn
Drake Law
Arbory Hill
Rome H
Abington

Auchinleck
Lugar
Logan
Wardlaw Hill
Stony Hill
Mount Stuart
Spango Water
Corsebank
Wanlock Water
Leadhills
Wellgrain Dod
Elvanfoot
Watchman Hill

Holmhead
Cumnock
Burnton
Skares
Dalblair
Halfmerk Hill
Cocker Hill
Carco
Wanlockhead
Green Lower 732
Glenochar
Tomont

Ochiltree
Craigdullyeart Hill
Lagrae
Kirkland
Willowgrain Hill
Lowther Hill
Mennock Pass

Carsgailoch Hill
Pathhead
Connel Park
Afton Bridgend
Celtic or Deil's Dike
Kirkconnel
Crawick
Drumbuie
Sanquhar
Mennock
Comb Law
Ballencleuch Law 692

Stannery Knowe
New Cumnock
Burnside
Laight
Hare Hill
Ulzieside
Eliock
Ardoch
Enterkinfoot
Durisdeer
Wedder Law
Whitesi

Clawfin
Maneight
Meikle Hill
Craigdarroch
Cruffell
Polgown
Cloud Hill
Glengenny Muir
Drumcruilton
Earncraig Hill
Gana Hill

Dalmellington
Windy Standard
Enoch Hill 569
Blacklorg Hill 681
Dalgonar
Wether Hill
Cairnkinna Hill
Breckonside
Drumcruilton

Todden Hill
Windy Standard 698
Countam
Colt Hill
DRUMLANRIG
Holm
Carronbridge
Dabton
Rashy Height
Queensb

Benbrack
Alhang
Cairnsmore of Carsphairn 797
Dodd Hill
Countam
Auchenbrack
Torbraehead
Auchenhessnane
Eccles
Thornhill
Burnhead
Gatelawbridge

Drumjohn
Lamloch
Brochloch
Garryhorn
Black Shoulder
Bail Hill
Benbuie
Bennan
Penpont
Clonrae
Tynron
Keir Mill
Closeburn
Croalchapel

Carsphairn
Knockgray
Bardennoch
Marscalloch Hill
Carroch
Wether Hill
Cornharrow Hill
Moniaive
Crawfordton
Kirkland
Keir Hills
Barndennoch
Blackwood
Glenhead

Castlemaddy
Dalshangan
Glencrosh
Craigdarroch
MAXWELTON
Crossford
Dalswinton Common
Ae Village

Forrest Lodge
Wether Hill
Castlefairn
Bogrie Hill 432
Sundaywell
Milton
Dunscore
Dalswinton
Friars Carse

Millfire 716
Burnhead
Knocknalling
Holmhead
Waterhead
Lochurr
Stroquhan
Speddoch
Gribto
Holywood
Locharbrig

Corriedoo
Bogue
Glenlee
St John's Town of Dalry
Balmaclellan
Blackcraig Hill
Waterhead
Craigenputtock
Knockla
Scroggie Hall
Slongaber
Skeoch Hill
New Bridge

**A**   **B**   **C**   **D**   **E**

0 1 2 3 4 5 10 15 kilometres
0 1 2 3 4 5 10 miles

**A**  **B**  **C**  **D**  **E**

Collie Law
Dun Law
Fountainhall
Scoured Rig
Edgarhope Wood
Greenlaw Moor
Choicelee
Warth
Whitsor
Horn
Torquhan
Inchkeith Hill
THIRLESTANE
Thirlestane
Westruther
Hule Moss
A6105
Fogo
Ladyki
Gala Bank
Lauder
Whiteburn
Houndslow
Greenlaw
Fogorig
Swinton
Upsettlington
Killochyett
Lauder Common
Purves Hall
Swintonmill
Simprim
Stow
Nether Blainslie
Legerwood
GREENKNOWE TOWER
Gordon
Howlaws
Orange Lane
Eccles
Leitholm
Torsonce
Birkhill
Huntlywood
Hume
Humehall
Legars
Lennel
Yardstone Knowe
Great Law
Caitha
Langshaw
Fans
B6397
Sweethope Hill
Hume
Stichill
Ednam
THE HIRSEL
Coldstream
Cornhill-on-Tweed
William Law
Buckholm
Earlston
MELLERSTAIN
Nenthorn
Hendersyde Park
Hadden
Carham
Wark
Branxto
Knowes Hill
TORWOODLEE
Glendearg
Redpath
Smailholm
Kelso
Maxwellheugh
Sprouston
Pressen
Downham
Galashiels
Gattonside
Drygrange
SMAILHOLM TOWER
FLOORS
Lempitlaw
Mindrum
Kilham
Thornylee
Ashiesteel
Caddonfoot
Melrose
Darnick
Newstead
Bemersyde
B6397
Roxburgh
Heiton
Blakelaw
Venchen Town Yetholm
Shotton
Westnew
Ashiesteel Hill
Boleside
PRIORWOOD
Newtown St Boswells
Clintmains
Manorhill
Trows
Kirk Yetholm
Coldsmouth Hill
Hethpool
Yair Hill Forest
Broomy Law
Peat Law
Lindean
Cauldshiels Hill
St Boswells
DRYBURGH
Bowden
Maxton
Rutherford
Bowmont Forest
Frogden
Linton Hill
Linton
White Law
Yarrowford
Broadmeadows
Selkirk
Bowhill
Philiphaugh
Midlem
Longnewton
Fairnington
Nisbet
Eckford
Morebattle
Crookedshaws Hill
The Curr
BOWHILL HOUSE
Fastheugh Hill
Clerklands
Riddell
Lilliesleaf
Ancrum
Gateshaw
Hownam Law
The Schil
Sourhope
Shaw's Hill
Akermoor Loch
Woll
Ashkirk
Chesters
Minto Hills
Minto
Newton
Lanton
Bonjedward
Crailing
Cessford
Crailinghall
Hownam Mains
Craik Moor
Mowhaugh
Langhope Burn
Hassendean
Horsleyhill
Clarilaw
Knowetownhead
Denholm
Bedrule
Hartrigge
MARY QUEEN OF SCOTS HOUSE
Jedburgh
Shibden Hill
Hownam
Drinkstone Hill
Newton
Esdale Law
Appletreehall
Ashybank
Dunion Hill
Hundalee
Langlee
Oxnam
Chatto
Swinside Hall
Swanlaws
Burnfoot
Borthwickshields
Wilton
Hawick
Rubers Law
Hallrule
Bairnkine
Mossburnford
Falla
Beefstand Hill
Windy Gyle
Loft Hill
Roberton
Branxholm Bridgend
Kirkton
Bonchester Bridge
Faw Hill
Mervinslaw
Brundeanlaws
Woden Law
Blindburn
Bell Hill
Borthwickbrae
Burnfoot
Branxholme
White Hill
Bonchester Hill
Hobkirk
Chesters
Jed Water
Huntford
Deerlee Knowe
Leithope Forest
Grindstone Law
Makendon
Woolbist Law
Shillmoor
Newmill
High Seat
Hott Hill
Cleuch Head
Wolfelee
Southdean
Carter Bar
Catcleugh Shin
Arks Edge
Hungry Law
Ravens Knowe
Crigdon Hill
Linshiels
Harwood on Teviot
Broadhaugh
Berryfell Hill
Wolfelee Hill
Hyndlee
Note o' the Gate
Green Law
Carter Fell
Catcleugh Rest
Windy Crag
Blackkip
ROMAN CAMP
Dryden Fell
Northhouse
Shankend
The Pike
Wyndburgh Hill
Wauchope Forest
Carlin Tooth
Byrness
DANGER
Corby Pike
Teviothead
Castleweary
Skelfhill Pen
Maiden Paps
Fanna Hill
Needs Law
Knox Knowe
Girdle Fell
Catcleugh
Redesdale Forest
Sills
Rochester
Harsey
Davy
Linhope
Cauldcleuch Head
Greatmoor Hill
Sandy Edge
Singdean
Hartshorn Pike
Kielderhead Moor
Ellis Crag
Toll
Mosspaul Hotel
Millstone Edge
Peel Fell
Oh Me Edge
Wether Lair
Blackman's Law
Hindhope Law
Redesdale
Wiss Hill
Tudhope Hill
Geordie's Hill
Saughtree Fell
Kielder Burn
Blackman's Law
Monkside
Emblehope Moor
Brownrigg Head
Blakeman's Law
Dargues
Hermitage
Din Fell
HERMITAGE
Saughtree
Foulmire Heights
Loch Knowe
Kielder
Earl's Seat
Padon Hill
Troughend
Hartsgarth Fell
Arnton Fell
Larriston
Toll
Wainhope
Highgreen Manor
Troughend Common
Pike Fell
Newlands
Steele Road
Dinlabyre
Castleton
Black Knowe
BORDER FOREST PARK
Kielder Forest
Highfield
Brownrigg Common
Blakehope Fell
Old Tow
Arkleton Hill
North Birny Fell
Wilson's Pike
Caplestone Fell
Hawkhope
White Hill
Falstone
Greenhaugh
West Woodburn
Hog Fell
Black Edge
Newcastleton Forest
Black Knowe
Rough Pike
Stannersburn
Bower
Charlton
Newcastleton
Tinnis Hill
Jock's Pike
The Rigg
Reeker Pike
Bolt's Law
Hope House
Heslyside
Bellingham
Langholm
Bruntshiel Hill
Kershopefoot
Blinkbonny Height
Bewcastle Fells
Gill Pike
Christianbury Crag
Sighty Crag
Black Knowe
Clintburn
Hetherington
Redesmo
Cauldside
Nook
Arthur Seat
Baileyhead
Kershope Forest
The Flatt
Padon Moor
Birtley

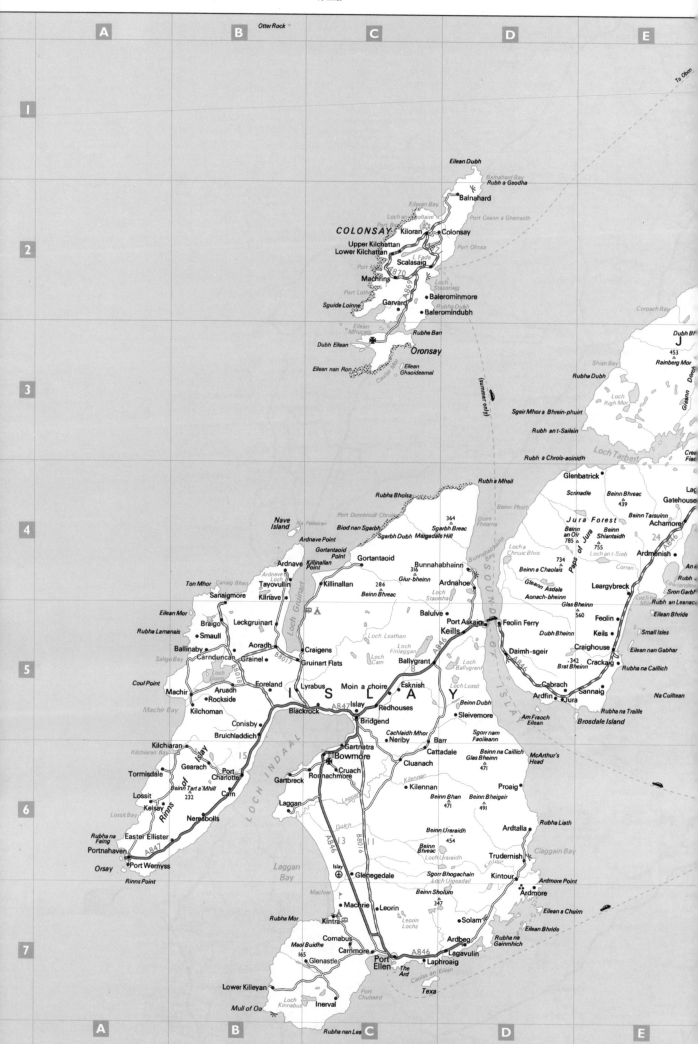

0 1 2 3 4 5    10    15 kilometres
0 1 2 3 4 5    10 miles

**A**   **B**   **C**   **D**   **E**

To Oban

Otter Rock

Eilean Dubh
Balnahard Bay
Rubh a Geodha
Kiloran Bay
Loch an t-Soltaire
Port Ceann a Gharraidh
COLONSAY   Kiloran   ● Colonsay
Port Mor
Upper Kilchattan
Lower Kilchattan
L Fada
Scalasaig
Machrins
Loch Staosnaig
Port Lobh
Balerominmore
Rubha Dubh
Garvard   ● Baleromindubh
Corpach Bay
Sguide Loinne
Eilean Nhucaig
Rubha Ban
Dubh BI
Dubh Eilean   J   453
Oronsay   Rainberg Mor
Eilean nan Ron   Shian Bay   Rubha Dubh
Caolas Mor   Eilean Ghaoideamal
Loch Righ Mor
(summer only)
Sgeir Mhor a Bhrein-phuirt
Rubh an t-Sailein
Rubh a Chrois-aoinidh   Loch Tarbert
Rubh Mhail   Glenbatrick   Cree Fiac
Scrinadle   Beinn Bhreac   439   Laç Gatehouse
Rubha Bholsa   JURA FOREST   Beinn Tarsuinn
Port Domhnuill Chruin   364   Doire Fhearna   Beinn an Oir 785   Beinn Shiantaidh 755   Achamore
Nave Island   Na Peileiran   Biod nan Sgarbh   Sgarbh Breac   Loch a Chnuic Bhric   734   Loch an t-Siob   24   A846
Ardnave Point   Sgarbh Dubh   Margadale Hill   Corran   Ardmenish   An
Gortantaoid Point   Gortantaoid   Beinn a Chaolais   Rubh
Ardnave   Killinallan Point   Bunnahabhainn   Gleann Asdale   Leargybreck   Sron Garbh
Ton Mhor   Carraig Bhan   Killinallan   316   Aonach-bheinn   Rubh an Leanac
Tayovullin   286   Ardnahoe   Glas Bheinn 560   Feolin   Eilean Bhride
Sanaigmore   Kilnave   Beinn Bhreac   Balulve   Feolin Ferry   Small Isles
Eilean Mor   Ardnave Loch   Loch Staoisha   Port Askaig   Dubh Bheinn   Keils
Braigo   Leckgruinart   Keills   342   Craighouse   Eilean nan Gabhar
Rubha Lamanais   ● Smaull   Daimh-sgeir   Brat Bheinn   Crackaig
Ballinaby   Aoradh   Craigens   Loch Leathan   Loch Finlaggan   Cabrach   Rubha na Caillich
Carnduncan   Grainel   B8017   Gruinart Flats   Loch Cam   Ballygrant   Ardfin   ● Jura   Na Cuiltean
Coul Point   Machir   Foreland   Lyrabus   Moin a choire   Esknish   Loch Lossit   Am Fraoch   Rubha na Traille
Aruadh   ● Rockside   I S L A Y   Blackrock   A847 Islay   Redhouses   Beinn Dubh   Eilean   Brosdale Island
Machir Bay   Kilchoman   Bridgend   Sleivemore
Conisby   Cachlaidh Mhor   Barr   Sgorr nam Faoileann
Bruichladdich   Gartnatra   Neriby   Beinn na Caillich   McArthur's Head
Kilchiaran   Bowmore   Cattadale   Glas Bheinn 471
Kilchiaran Bay   ● Cruach   Cluanach   Kilennan   Beinn Bhan 471   Beinn Bheigeir 491   Proaig
Gearach   Port Charlotte   Ronnachmore   Rubha Liath
Tormisdale   Beinn Tart a'Mhill 232   Gartbreck   Kilennan   Ardtalla
Lossit   Cam   Laggan   Beinn Uraraidh 454   Trudernish   Claggain Bay
Kelsay   Laggan   Beinn Bhreac   Loch Uraraidh   Kintour
Nereabolls   Duich   Kintour   Ardmore Point
Rubha na Faing   Rinns of Islay   A846   B8016   Sgorr Bhogachain   Kintour   Ardmore
Easter Ellister   Islay   Beinn Sholum 347   Eilean a Chuirn
Portnahaven   Laggan Bay   Glenegedale   Loch Uigeadail   Solam   Eilean Bhride
Orsay   Port Wemyss   Machrie   Leorin Lochs   Rubha na Gainmhich
Rinns Point   Rubha Mor   Machrie   Leorin   Ardbeg
Maol Buidhe   Kintra   Lagavulin
Lower Killeyan   165   Cornabus   A846   Laphroaig
Glenastle   Carnmore   Port Ellen   The Ard
Mull of Oa   Loch Kinnabus   Inerval   Port Chubaird   Texa   Caolas an Eilein
Rubha nan Lea

**1**  **2**  **3**  **4**  **5**  **6**  **7**

**A**   **B**   **C**   **D**   **E**

0 1 2 3 4 5    10    15 kilometres
0 1 2 3 4 5    10 miles

**Grid references:** A B C D E — 1 2 3 4 5 6 7

Ardgenavan · Cairndow · Glen Kinglas · Binnein an Fhidhleir · Ben Vane · Inveruglas · A82 · Stronachlachar · Strath Gartney · Loch Katrine · Edra · Ben Ledi

Drishaig · Ardkinglas Ho. · Glen · Beinn Dhubh · Glen Arklet · Inversnaid Hotel · Glasahoile · Ellen's Isle · Ben An · Cnoc nan Sitheag · Co

Aray · Laglingarten · Stone Point · St Catherines · Ardno · Rest and be thankful · Beinn Ime · A'Chrois · Cruach Tairbeirt · Rowchoish · Comer · Ben Venue · The Trossachs · Brig o' Turk · Duncraggan · A821

Hazelbank · Cruach nan Capull · Monevechadan · Ben Arthur · The Cobbler · Succoth · Arrochar · Stuckgowan · Ben Lomond · Blairuskinmore · Glen Dubh · Kinlochard · Achray Forest · Invertrossachs

Creggans · Strachur · Drimsynie · Lochgoilhead · Cnoc Coinnich · Ardgartan Forest · The Brack · Ardmay · (NTS) 974 · Dukes Pass · Milton · Port Menteith

Mid Letter · Glenslvan · Ballemeanoch · Corrow · Coilessan · Craggan · Ben Reoch 681 · Rowardennan Lodge · QUEEN ELIZABETH FOREST · Blairhullichan · Duchray · Aberfoyle · Braeval · Malling · Lake of Menteith

Balliemore · Inveroaden · Glenbranter · Carnach Mor · Beinn Bheula · Glenmallan · Glen Douglas · Doune Hill · Inverbeg · 596 Beinn Uird · Loch Ard Forest · Gartmore · Cobleland

Glenshellish · Beinn Dubhain · Sgurr a' Choinnich · Finnart · Beinn Eich · Culag · Ross Point · Beinn Bhreac · Duchray Water · Auchentroig · Buch

Cuilmuich · Corran · Glen Luss · Uray · Inchlonaig · REGIONAL · Ward Burn · A811 · Gartachoil

Stuck · Carrick · Camstraddan · Luss · Inchtavannach · Cashell · Milarrochy · Pass of Balmaha · Garadhban Forest · Gard

Beinn Bheag 618 · Cruach a Bhuic · Creachan Mor · Garelochhead · Glenalt · Beinn Ruisg · Aldochlay · Inchconnachan (NTS) · Inchcruin · Balmaha · Milton · Balfron

Bernice · Ardnahein · Private Road · Belmore · Beinn Tharsuinn · Auchinvennal · Shantron · Rossdhu House · Creinch · Torrinch · Inchcailloch · Drymen · Boquhan · A875

Sron Mhor 742 · Barnacabber · Coylet · Mambeg · Balernock · Shandon · Blairnairn · 593 · Inchmoan · LOCH LOMOND · Inchmurrin · Ross Priory · Duncryne · Gartness · Killearn

Clach Bheinn · Stronlonag · Ardentinny · Stronchullin Hill · Meikle Rahane · Linnburn · Blarglas · Lorn · Gartocharn · Caldarvan · Auchencarroch · Dumgoyne · Strathblane

Benmore · Uig · Cnoc a' Mhadaidh · Ardpeaton · A814 · Inverlauren · Dumfin · Arden · Caldarvan Loch · Earl's Seat 578 · Blairquhosh · Dumgoyne Hill · Strathb

Ballochyle Hill · Ardbeg · Gairletter Point · Clynder · Blairvadach · Daligan · BALLOCH CASTLE · Devil's Pulpit · Auchineck · Moss · Carbeth · Blanefield · Strathb

Glenlean · Ballochyle · Kilmun · Strone · Rosneath · Rhu · Stroul · HILL HOUSE (NTS) · A811 · A809 · Dumgoyne · Mugdock

Clachaig · Sandbank · Ardnadam · Cove · Hartfield · Camsail · Helensburgh · Craigendoran · Balloch · Jamestown · Dumbarton Muir · Carbeth

Glenkin · Dunloskin · Hunter's Quay · Kilcreggan · Camis Eskan · Colgrain · Alexandria · Bonhill · Milngavie · Balder

Inverchaolain · Bishop's Seat · Kirn · Gourock · GREENOCK · Ardmore · Cardross · Renton · Townend · Loch Humphrey · Kilpatrick Hills · Bearsden

Dunoon · 522 · West Bay · Cloch Point · Castle Levan · PORT GLASGOW · Crosslet · DUMBARTON · Milton · Bowling · Cochno · Edinbarnet · Dougals

Bullwood · Ardhallow · Chrisswell · Lurg Moor · Langbank · Old Kilpatrick · Duntocher · Drumchapel · Bishop

Blairbuie · Corlarach Hill · Beinn Ruadh · Ardgowan · Inverkip · Loch Thom · Strath Gryfe · Auchenbothie · Bishopton · Erskine · CLYDEBANK · Maryhill

Knockdow · Achafour · Dunan · Wemyss Bay · Leap Moor · Gryfe Reservoirs · Caimcurran Hill · Kilmacolm · Houston · Georgetown · Inchinnan · Yoker

Ardmaleish · Innellan · Corkney Top 441 · Creuch Hill · Duchal · Quarrier's Homes · Crosslee · Glasgow · Renfrew · Govan

Ardbeg · Skelmorlie · Black Fell · Duchal Moor · Bridge of Weir · Weaver's Cottage (NTS) · Carruthmuir · Linwood · PAISLEY

Bogany Point · Craigmore · Orcadia · North Burnt Hill · Calder Dam · Queenside Muir 522 · MUIRSHIEL · Kilbarchan · Johnstone · Elderslie · Pollok · Pollokshaws

Ascog · Kerrycroy · Noddsdale · Rowantree Hill · Netherhall · Hill of Stake · Misty Law · Slaty Law · Howwood · Johnstone Castle · Millikenpark · Nitshill

Grenach · Mountstuart · Tomont End · Largs · Gogo Water · Black Law · CASTLE SEMPLE WATER · Whittliemuir · Midton Loch · The Peesweep · Barrhead · Thornliebank

Largs Bay · Blairpark · Irish Law · Lochwinnoch · Corkindale Law · GLENIFFER BRAES · Neilston · Clarkston · Newton Mearns

Great Cumbrae · Muirhead Resr · Whitehill · Kilbirnie · Woodside · Lochlands Hill · Hall · Neilston Pad · Harelaw Dam · Malletsheugh · Mearns

Millport · Fairlie · Camphill Resr · 387 · South Howrat · Beith · Caldwell · Windy Yet · Corsehouse · Eaglesham

Kilchattan Bay · Ore Terminal · Kaim Hill · Cock Law · Knockendon Resr · Glengarnock · Barrmill · Lugton · Long Loch · Ballageich Hill 330 · Polnoon

Torr Mor · Inner Brigurd Point · Hunterston · The Den · Highfield · Burnhouse · Dunlop · Kingsford · Kingswells · Lochgoin · Melowther Hill

Little Cumbrae Island · Gull Point · Portencross · Farland Head · Gill · Giffordland · Dalry · Blair · Auchentiber · Corsehill · Dunwan Dam

West Kilbride · Seamill · Dalgarven · Montgreenan · Stewarton · Fenwick · Waterside · CUNNINGHAME

Ardrossan · Stevenston · Kilwinning · Montgreenan · Cunninghamhead · Knockentiber · Kilmaurs · Moscow · Pley Moss

Horse Isle · Saltcoats · Irvine · KILMARNOCK · Darvel

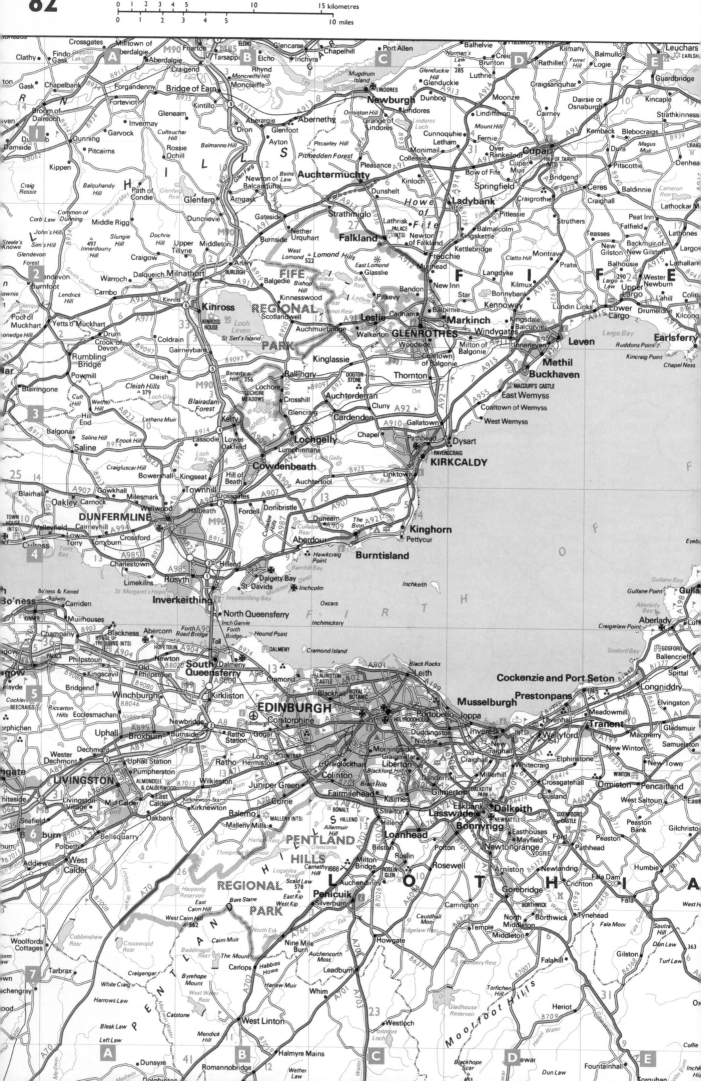

A B C D E

Andrews Bay

St Andrews

Kinkell Ness
Buddo Ness
Boarhills
Babbet Ness
Prior Muir
aldy
B9131
Stravithie
Dunino
Kingsbarns
Cambo Ness
North Carr
Balcomie
Tullybothy Craigs
Wormistone
Fife Ness
chty
Airdrie
A9171
Lochty Railwy
Carnbee
Spalefield
Crail
West Ness
angemuir
Kilrenny
Innergellie
Cellardyke
Anstruther
Pittenweem
St
Monans

North Ness

Isle of May
South Ness

R T H

R

Fidra
Craigleith
Bass Rock
Lamb

North Berwick
A198
St Baldred's Boat
North Berwick
Law
Auldhame
TANTALLON
IRLETON
(NTS)
Kingston
Whitekirk
St Baldred's Cradle
Tyne Mouth
rem
East Fortune
TYNINGHAME
HOUSE
oswells
Tyninghame
JOHN MUIR
Dunbar
Preston
West Barns
Belhaven
East Linton
PRESTON
MILL (NTS)
Broxburn
Barns Ness
taneford
HAILES
Biel
1296
Skateraw
Skatraw Harbour
eton Hills
Traprain
Pitcox
Spott
Brunt Hill
Thorntonloch
Haddington
Stenton
Innerwick
Reed Point
Rapple
Halls
Dry Burn
Bilsdean
NOXLOVE
Whitelaw
Hill
Garvald
Cocklaw Hill
Cockburnspath
Siccar Point
FAST CASTLE
olton
MUNRAW ABBEY
Bransly Hill
Oldhamstocks
Wheat Stack
Telegraph Hill
St Abb's Head
(NTS)
Gifford
Carfrae
Dunbar Common
HILLS
Monynut Edge
Ecclaw
Meikle
Black Law
Lumsdaine
Cross Law
Coldingham
Loch
Northfield
St Abbs
Danskine
Clints Dod
Ecclaw Hill
Coldingham
Moor
Coldingham
Bay
B6355
Rangeley
Kip
Heart Law
Blackburn Rig
Grantshouse
12
PRIORY
Longyester
Newlands Hill
GAMELSHIEL
Laughing
Law
Houndwood
A1107
Eyemouth
mer Law
528
N
Whiteadder
Resr
Penshiel
Hill
Abbey St Bathans
A1 20
Cairncross
Burnmouth
Hopes
Resr
MERMUIR
535
Cranshaws
EDIN'S HALL
BROCH
Drakemire
Horseley Hill
Marygold
Reston
Ayton
Ayton
Hill
Crib Law
Seenes Law
Meikle
Says Law
Meikle Law
Ellemford
Cranshaws Hill
Cockburn Law
Preston
Auchencrow
Millerton Hill
Hilton Bay
Hunt Law
495
Wrunk
Law
Longformacus
Lintlaw
B6437
Lamberton
Lamberton
Beach
Hogs Law
Blythe
Edge
Dye Water
B6355
Chirnsidebridge
Chirnside
A6105
Foulden
Clappers
Halidon
Hill
1333
per's Hea
Watch Water
Resr
Dirrington
Great Law
MANDERSTON
Edrom
Whiteadder Water
Hutton
Paxton
Berwick-upon-Tweed
Needles Eye
A697
Dirrington
Little Law
Duns
Allanton
B6461
Tweedmouth
Scoured
Rig
B6456
Gavinton
Cheeklaw
Whitelaw
Blackadder
Sunwick
Whitsome
Fishwick
East Ord
Spittal
Choicelee
Greenlaw
Moor
Polwarth
A6112
Horndean
Longridge Towers
THIRLESTANE
Thirlestane
Wes er
Fogo
Hule Moss
A6105
Fogorig
Swinton
Ladykirk
NORHAM
Thorntonpark
Thornton
Murton
Scremers

A B C D E

1
2
3
4
5
6
7

0 1 2 3 4 5     10     15 kilometres
0 1 2 3 4 5     10 miles

A          B          C          D          E

1

HEBRIDES

To Lochboisdale

Rubh 'Leam na La

To Castlebay

Ardnam

2

Eag na Maoile     Eilean Mor
Rubha Mor     Rubha Sgor innis
Rubh a Bhinnein     Bousd     Loch     Sorisdale
Torastan     Fada     Bagh na Coille

Cliad Bay     Arnabost
Grishipoll Bay     Grishipoll     73
Clabhach     Bagh Feisdlum
Ballyhaugh     Loch
Hogh Bay     104     Cliad
Totamore     C O L L     Eilean nam Muc
Arinagour
Totronald     Loch Eatharna
Uig     Caliach Point     La
Arileod     Acha     Sunipol     Mornish
Calgary Point     Eilean Ornsay     Port na     Mornish
Crossapol     Gorton     Cruach Sleibhe     166
3     Port Mine     Friesland     Port na h-eithir     Rubha nan Oirean
Gunna     Crossapol     Bay     Rubha Fasachd
Bay     Port a Mhurain     Soa     Ensay
Urvaig     Treshnish Point     Treshnish     C
Miodar     Beinn Duill
Balephetrish     Caoles     Rubha Dubh     191     Cr
Hill     Ruaig     Port Ban     Rubh a Chaoil     Reudle
The     B8069     Brock     Rubh an t-Suibhein
Green     Balephetrish Bay     Soa     Rubha Lieth     Gott Bay     Cairn na Burgh More     Cairn na Burgh Beg     LOCH
4     T I R E E     Scarinish     Fladda     Rubha     na Sroine
Kilkenneth     5     Tiree     Sgeir a Chaisteil     Eilean Dioghlum     Gometra
Crossapol     Heanish     Rubha Maol     Gometra
Saundaig     B8065     Heylipoll     Baugh     5     na Mine     Eol
Barrapoll     2     Hynish     Lunga     Maisgeir
Balemartine     Bay     Treshnish Isles     Little
Balephuil     B8067     Colonsay
Hynish     Bac Mor or
Dutchman's Cap
Bac Beag

Staffa     Eilean Dubh
5     Fingal's     (NTS)
Cave     The Causeway

Erisgeir

Rubha na

Aird na

Reidh Eilean     Eilean     Eilean     Carraig Mhi
Annraidh
Eilean     Rubha nan Cearc
6     Chalbha     Dun     Kintra
Port an Duine Mhairbh     (NTS)     Beinn Chladan     Eorabus
Iona     Fionnphort     Loch na
Stac an Aoineidh     Ruanaich     Aridhglas     A849     Lathaich
Rubha na Carraig-geire     Fidden     Bunessa
R O S S     O
Knockvologan     Ardalanish
Soa Island     Erraid     Torr Fada     Ardchiavaig
Eilean Dubh     Aird Mor     Port
Eilean a Chalmain     Mor

Eilean Mor
Ruadh Sgeir     Rubh' Ardalan
7     Torran Rocks     Dearg Sgeir
Na Torrain
West Reef     Torran Sgoilte
McPhail's Anvil     Sgeir Ghobhlach

Otter Rock

A          B          C          D          E

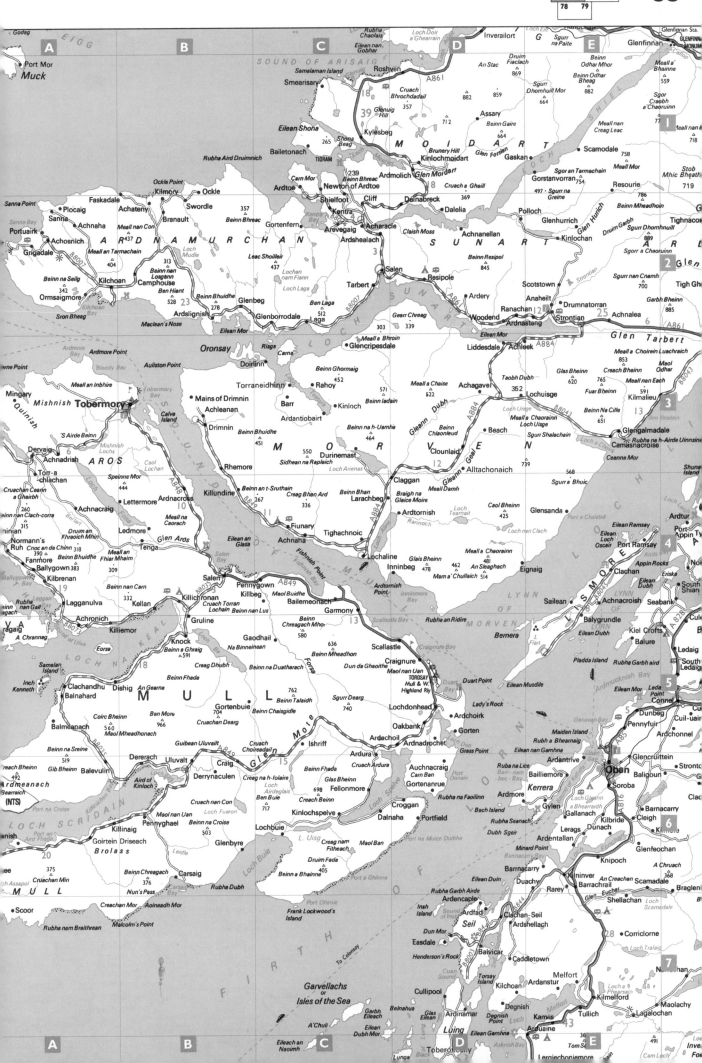

0 1 2 3 4 5    10    15 kilometres
0 1 2 3 4 5    10 miles

Glenfinnan Sta. · Glenfinnan · GLENFINNAN MONUMENT · Kinlocheil · Locheilside Station · Loch Eil Centre · Muirshearlich · Killiechonate · Roybridge · Braes o' Lochaber · Murlaggan · Roug

Drumfern · Garvan · Duisky · Blaich · Achaphubuil · Corpach · Banavie · Torcastle · Torlundy · Tom an Teine · Beinn Chlianaig · Fersit

Camusnagaul · Trislaig · Caol · Inverlochy · Fort William · Claggan · Achintee · Killiechonate Forest · Stob Coire Claurigh · Stob Coire Easain · Chno De

Meall a' Bhainne · Sgor Craobh a' Chaoruinn · Meall nan Damh · Meall an Fheidh · Corrlarach · Sgurr Lubhair · Goirtean a Chladaich · Druimarbin · Blarmachfoldach · Polldubh · Achriabhach · Ben Nevis 1344 · Carn Dearg · Aonach Mor · Aonach Beag · Sgurr Choinnich Mor · Meall a' Bhuirich · Garbh Bheinn

 Conaglen · Glen Scaddle · Tighnacomaire · Creagbheitheachain · Aryhoulan · Corrychurrachan · Lundavra · Blar a Chaorainn · Mullach nan Coirean · An Garbhanach · Mamore Forest · Binnein Beag · Luibeilt · Corrour Sta.

Ardgour · Bheinn Bhan · Sallachan · Clovullin · Corran · Keppanach · Onich · North Ballachulish · Ballachulish · Kentallen · Glencoe · Bridge of Coe · Kinlochmore · Kinlochleven · Caolasnacon · Glas Bheinn · Leum Uilleim

Glen Gour · Tigh Ghlinnegabhar · Gearradh · Inversanda · Rubh a' Bhaid Bheithe · Ballachulish · Pap of Glencoe · Aonach Eagach · Devil's Staircase · Beinn a Chrulaiste · Meall Bhalach · Black Corries · Stob na Cruaiche

Glen Tarbert · Rubha Mor · Auchindarroch · Glenduror · Glen Duror Forest · Ossian's Cave · The Three Sisters · Bidean Nam Bian 1150 · Buachaille Etive Beag · Buachaille Etive Mor · King's House Hotel · Rannoch Mo

Glengalmadale · Eilean Balnagowan · Inshaig · Keil · Dalnatrat · Achvlair · Salachail · Meall Lighiche · Sgor na h-Ulaidh · Royal Forest · Lochan na h-Achlaise

Lurignich · Polanach · North Dallens · Fasnacloich · Elleric · Glenure · Barnamuc · Beinn Fhionnlaidh · Glen Etive · Dalness · Clach Leathad · Black Mount

Ardtur · Port Appin · Tynribbie · Kinlochlaich · Glasdrum · Invercreran · Taravocan · Druimavuic · Inver · Invercharnan · Glenceitlein · Coileitir · Stob Ghabhar · Achallader · Beinn a Chreachain

North Shian · Dallachoilish · Creach Bheinn · Beinn Sguliard · Gualachulain · Kinlochetive · Stob Coir an Albannaich · Black Mount · Clashgour · Inveroran Hotel · Beinn an Dothaidh

Barcaldine · Achacha · Culcharan · Beinn Molurgainn · Ben Starav · Glas Bheinn Mhor · Beinn nan Aighenan · Beinn Suidhe · Bridge of Orchy · Beinn Dorain

Kiel Crofts · Balure · Ledaig · South Ledaig · Achnacairn · Dail · Cadderlie · Ardmaddy · Beinn nan Lus · Meall Buidhe · Beinn a Chuirn · Beinn Inverveigh · Auch

Connel · Dunbeg · Culnadalloch · Achnacloich · Airds Point · Inverliver · Acharn · Beinn Mhic-Mhonaidh · Arichastlich · Clifton · Tyndrum · Auchtertyre

Pennyfuir · Cuil-uaine · Dallnamac · Balure · Bonawe · Craig · Glennoe · Beinn Lurachan · Beinn Udlaidh · Arrivain · Beinn Chuirn · Beinn Bhreac-liath

Ardchonnel · Balindore · Taynuilt · Bonawe Quarries · Beinn Eunaich · Beinn a Chochuil · Duiletter · Achnafalnich · Cononish · Auchreoch · Inverherive · Crianlarich

Glencruitten · Strontoiller · Glenamachrie · Fanans · Ben Cruachan · Drishaig · Stronmilchan · Edendonich · Strath of Orchy · Inverlochy · Glen Lochy · Ben Lui · Beinn Dubhchraig · Ben Oss

Baligoun · Clachadow · Cruach Ardeny · Tailor's Leap · Pass of Brander · Falls of Cruachan · Lochawe · Dalmally · Meall nan Tighearn · Fiarach

Barnacarry · Beinn Ghlas · Shellachan · Trevine · Barachander · Ardanaiseig · Inishail · Ardteatle · Barran · Beinn Bhalgairean · Beinn Bhoidheach

Glenfeochan · A Chruach · Midmuir · Musdale · Kilchrenan · Annat · Hayfield · North Port · Inistrynich · Achlian · Cladich · Accurrach · Ceann Garbh

Scamadale · Braglenbeg · Beinn Dearg · Auchachenna · Coillaig · Ardbrecknish · Portsonachan · Taynafead · Shira · Beinn Bhuidhe · Meall an Fhudair · Inverarnan

Corriclorne · Lochna Sreinge · Inverinan · Inverinan Forest · Ballimeanoch · Tullich · Ladyfield · Drimlee · Elrigbeg · Glen Shira · Achadunan · Garabal · Ben Glas

Maolachy · Lagalochan · Drissaig · Cruach Mhor · Stuc Scardan · Clachan Hill · Stuckindroin · Doune · Beinn a' Choin · Ardlui · Ardleish

Dalavich · Ardchonnell · Portinnisherrich · High Balantyre · Sallachry · Kilblaan · Ardgenavan · Clachan · Carndow · Ben Vorlich · Ardvorlich · Stronach

Inverliever Forest · Eredine · Eredine Forest · Inveraray · Cairndow · Ardkinglas Ho. · Glen Kinglas · Ben Vane · Inveruglas

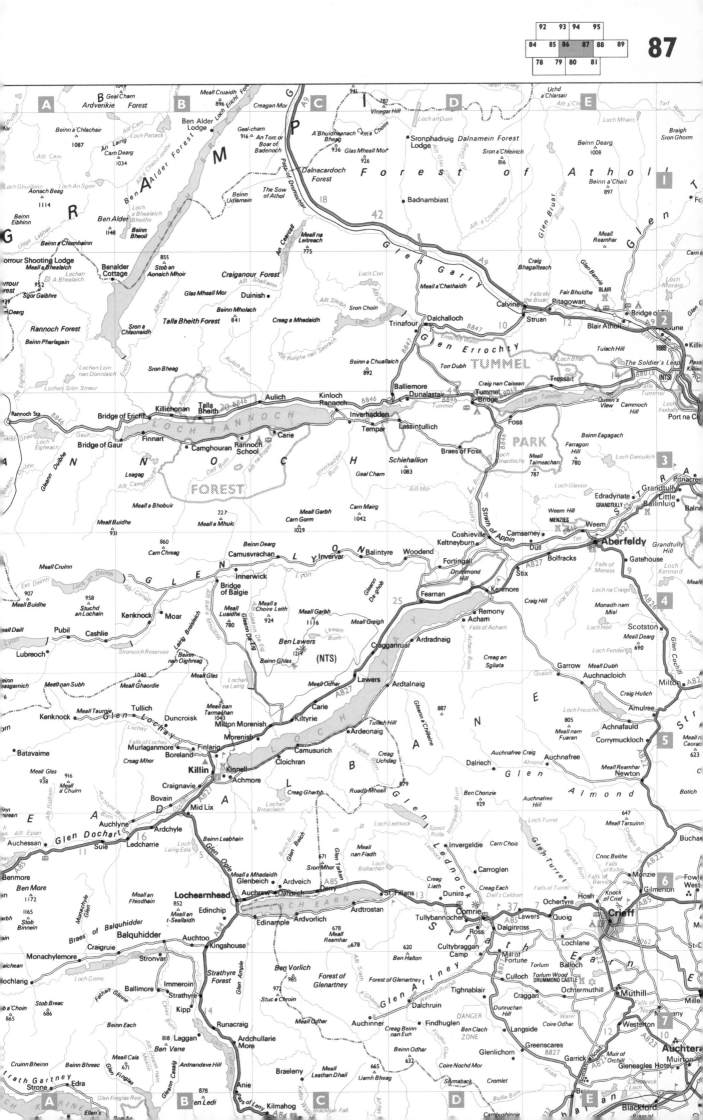

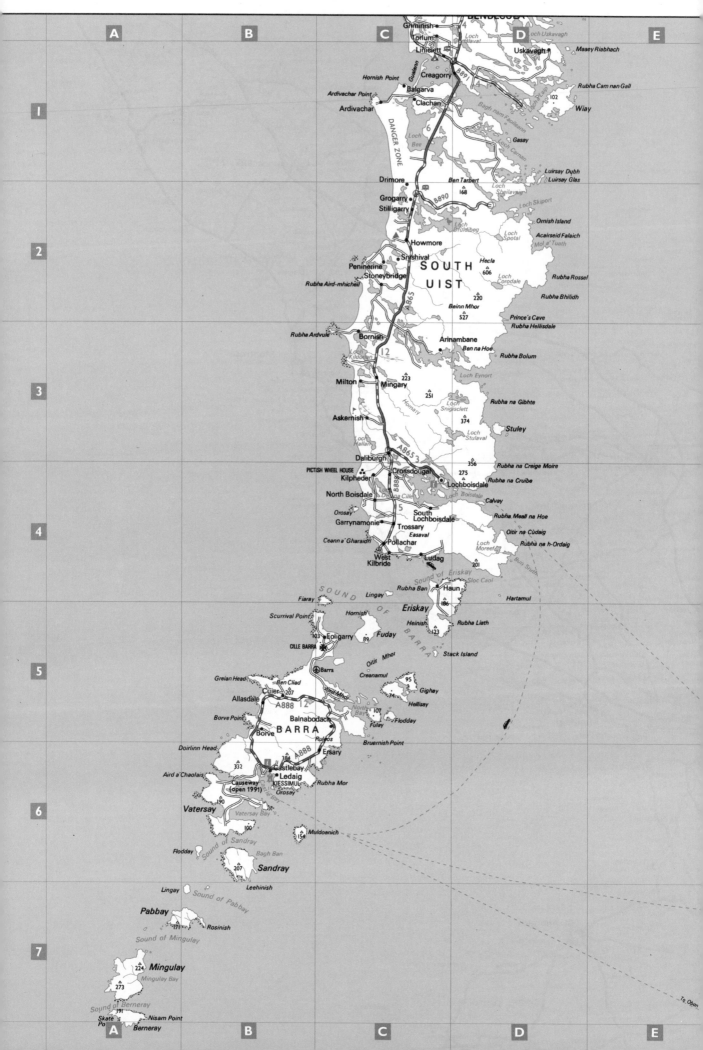

A B C D E

A850

Husabost
Feriniquarrie Totaig
Milova
Colbost
Beinn na Creiche
Waterstein Head 295
Skinidin
DUNVEGAN
Dunvegan Kilmuir
Lonmore
Glen Dale
B884
Ben Horneval 264
Edinbain
Bernisdale
Tote
Carbost
B8081
Borve
A850
Ben Uigshader 246
Skeabost
Beinn a'Chearcaill 552
Loch Fada

Neist Point
Ben Corkeval
Healaval More
Macleod's Table North 469
Roskhill
Roag
Orbost
A863
Caroy
Ben Sca 271
Ben Aketil 265
Cruachan Beinn a'Chearcaill 208
Loch Ravag
Drumuie
Glengrasco
Ben Eassie
Rubha na Airde Glai

Ramasaig
Hoe Rape
The Hoe 231
Lorgill
Healaval Beg
Macleod's Table South 488
Harlosh
Balmore
Harlosh Point
Osdale
Glen Ose
Beinn na Cloiche 230
Loch Connan
Am Maol 212
Ben Grasco
Beinn na Greine 417
Glenmore
A850
Portree
Udair
Ben Tianavaig 413
Camastianavaig

Hoe Point
Ben Connan 244
Beinn na Boineid 366
Harlosh Island
Loch Bracadale
Tarner Island
Ullinish
Bracadale
Struan
Coillore
S K Y E
Ben Duagrich 304
Mugeary
Stroc-bheinn 396
Beinn Totaig
Glen Varragill

An Dubh Sgeir
Ben Idrigill 340
MacLeod's Maidens
Idrigill Point
Wiay
Oronsay
Ardtreck Point
Portnalong
Fernilea
Loch Harport
Roineval 439
Meall an t'Fhuarain
A850
Ben 444
The Braes
Peinchorran

Rubha nan Clach
Arnaval 396
Carbost
Drynoch
A863
Glen Drynoch
Broc-bheinn
Glamaig 775
Sco

Gleann Oraid
Talisker
B8009
Beinn Bhreac 369
Allt Dearg Mor
Glen Sligachan

Talisker Bay
Stockval 416
Biod Mor 383
Beinn a'Bhraghad 459
Coire na Creiche
Bruach na Frithe
Sgurr nan Gillean 965
Marsco
Sligachan

Biod Ruadh
Beinn Bhreac 447
Beinn Staic 410
Sgurr Thuilm 879
Sgurr nan Gillean 958
Harta Corrie
Druim Hain

Sgurr Mor
Loch Eynort
Sgurr na Banachdich 965
Cuillin Hills
Loch Coruisk

An Dubh-sgeir
An Cruachan 435
Sgurr Dearg 986
Sgurr Alasdair 993
Sgurr na Str

Bualintur
Glenbrittle
Culnamean
Beinn an Eoin 312
Sgurr nan Eag 926
Gars-bheinn 894
Sgurr na Stri 495
Cam

Rubha Thearna Sgurr
Ceann na Beinne
Loch Brittle

Rubh' an Dunain
Beinn Bhreac 141
LOCH SCAV

Leac nam Faoileann
Soay
Mol-chlach
Elgol

C U I L L I N
Prince Charles's Cave
Rubh' Aonghais
Eilean na h Airde

**CANNA**
Camas Thubernish
Compass Hill
Carn a Ghaill 211
A'Chill 140
Garrisdale Point
(NTS)
Sron Ruail
Canna Harbour
An Steidh
Sanday
SOUND OF CANNA

Rubha Shamhnan Insir
Camas Pliasgaig

Kilmory
Sgaorishal
Mullach Mor 304
278
Rubha na Roinne

Guirdil Bay
388
Bloodstone Hill
National Nature Reserve
Humla
A'Bhrideanach
Orval 571
KINLOCH
Kinloch

**R U M**
**(RHUM)**
263
591
Hallival 723
Askival

Garbh Sgeir
Oigh-sgeir
Harris
Ruinsival 528
Ainshival 781
764
812
Stac nam Faoileann

SOUND OF RUM
Rubha nam Meirleach
Cleadale
Rubha nan Tri Chlach
299

To Mallaig (summer only)
Rubha an Fhasaidh
Rubha an 315
**EIGG**

SEA OF
To Oban
THE
HEBRIDES
An Sgurr 393
Kil an
Galmisdale

Eilean nan Each
Godag
D ish 'Leam na Laraich 138
Port
Muck

A B C D E

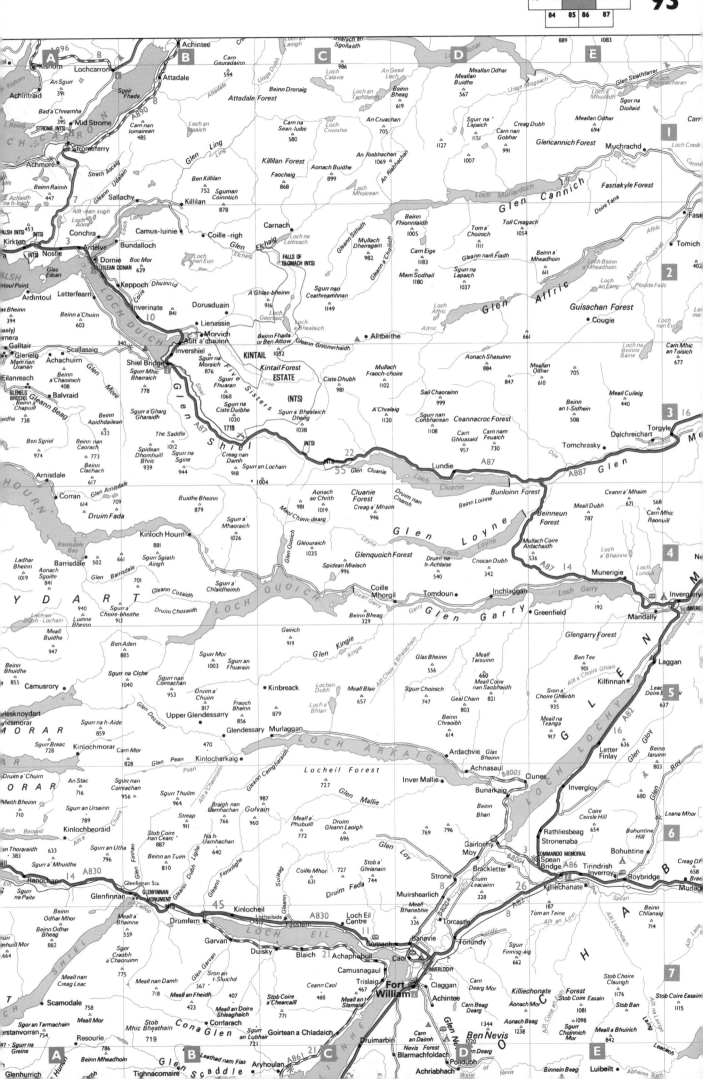

A map of the Cairngorms / Strathspey region of Scotland, with grid references A–E across and 1–7 down.

Place names and features shown include:

Fisherton, Drumine, Cawdor, Piperhill, Culcharry, Littlemill, Forres, Darnaway Forest, Presley, Logie, Tomnamoon, Romach Hill, Ardoch, Craigroy, Meikle, Cairn Uish, The Kell

Tornagrain, Newton, Dalcross, Croy, Dallaschyle, Clephanton, Urchany, Shaw Hill, Relugas, Hill of Tomechole, Craigroy

Cantraywood, Easter Galcantray, Achindown, Redburn, Mount Ferness, Tomdow, Carn Ghiubhais, Priestfield, Upper Knockando, Cardow

Balloch, Culloden Forest, Cantray, Kirkton of Barevan, Clunas, Bruachmary, Carn Maol, Daltra, Cairn Duhie, Carn Kitty, Carn Shalag, Knockando, Carron

Castletown, Saddle Hill, Dalroy, Carn-a'Chrassie, Dulsie, Milltown, Sliabh Bainnech, Larig Hill, Paul's Hill, Scootmore Forest, Marypark, Belleheiglash

Craggie, Daviot, Beinn Bhuidhe Mhor, Carn nan tri-tighearnan, Daless, Streens, Aitnoch, Hill of Aitnoch, Dava, Carn Rughe an Uain, Gallow Hill, Lynemore, Bridge of Avon

Moy, Beinn Bhreac, Meall a' Bhreacraibh, Lochindorb, Dava Moor, Carn na Loine, Advie, Toremore, Craigroy, Delchirach, Cairnacay

Meall Mor, Ruthven, Inveren, Balvraid, Carn an t-Sean-liathanaich, Anaboard, Upper Derraid, Auchnagallin, Knock of Auchnahannet, Lettoch, Duiar, Craggan, Drumin

Tomatin, Findhorn Bridge, Carn a' Choire Mhoir, Beinn Mhor, Cameroy, Creag Liath, Cottartown, Glaschoil, Tomvaich, Delliefure, Carn a' Ghille Chearr, Glenlivet, Shenva

Woodend, Beinn Bhreac, Corrievorrie, Clune, Carn nam Bain-tighearna, Achnahannet, Tullochgribban, Grantown-on-Spey, Cromdale, Haughs of Cromdale, Carn Eachie

Daltomach, Bogroy, Carrbridge, Slochd, Duthil, Skye of Curr, Dulnain Bridge, Gaich, Speybridge, Congash, Hills of Cromdale, Carn Daimh

Dalnahaitnach, Drumuillie, Cullachie, Nethy Bridge, Sliemore, Dirdhu, Bridge of Brown, Knockandhu, Glenconglass, Fodderletter

Dalmigavie, Eil, Caggan, Boat of Garten, Kinveachy, Dell Lodge, Lainchoil, Baddoch, Tom an t-Suidhe Mhoir, Tomintoul, Findron, Lagganvoulin

Carn Caol, Carn Sleamhuinn, Avielochan, Auchgourish, Abernethy Forest, Tore Hill, Aundorach, Braes of Abernethy, Delnabo, Badnafrave, Blairnamarrow

Cnoc Fraing, Carn Dearg Mor, Geal Charn Mor, Granish, Aviemore, Inverdruie, Loch Pityoulish, Craiggowrie, Tulloch, GLENMORE FOREST PARK, Geal Charn, Delavorar, Torbain

An Sguabach, Doune, Coylumbridge, The Queen's Forest, Glenmore Lodge, Mam Suim, An Lurg, Big Garvoun, Inchrory

A' Bhuidheanach, Carn an Fhreiceadain, An Suidhe, Kinrara, Rothiemurchus, Loch Garmha, Loch Morlich, Castle Hill, Bynack More, Forest of Glenavon, Loch Builg

Kincraig, Feshiebridge, Balnespick, Creag Follais, Carn Eilrig, CAIRNGORM MOUNTAINS, Cairn Gorm, Stob an t-Sluichd, Ben Avon, Culardoch

Kingussie, Newtonmore, Ruthven, Drumguish, Killiehuntly, Tolvah, Achlean, Sgoran Dubh Mor, Sgor Gaoith, Cairn Toul, Ben Macdui, Derry Cairngorm, Beinn a'Bhuird, Creag an Dail Bheag, Carn Liath

Lynaberack, Meall Buidhe, Baileguish, Carn Ban, Monadh Mor, The Devil's Point, Carn a'Mhaim, Carn Crom, Glen Quoich, Invercauld Forest, Meall Gorm, Braemar

Glen Tromie, Glen Feshie, Meall Dubhag, Mullach Clach a'Bhlair, Beinn Bhrotain, Sgor Mor, Mar Forest, Allanaquoich, Mar Lodge, Tomintoul, Invercauld Bridge

Gaick Lodge, Gaick Forest, Loch an t-Seilich, Carn an Fhidhleir Lorgaidh, An Sgarsoch, Carn Bhac, Glen Ey Forest, An Socach, Sgor Mor, Carn an Tuirc, Newbigging, Loch Callater, Creag nan Gabhar

Braeriach, Ben Macdui, Cairngorms Nature Reserve, Glen Dee, Linn of Dee, Carn Liath, The Colonel's Bed, Glen Callater, Carn of Claise

0 1 2 3 4 5 10 15 kilometres
0 1 2 3 4 5 10 miles

# WESTERN ISLES

**A** **B** **C** **D** **E**

Gasker

Fof Harris
489 679 656
Oreva 660
Arda
Beaga 412 Govick
Horsanish Cleiseval
Rubha Bhuic Amhuinnsuidhe 511
Ru-scu 12
Taransay Glorigs Soay Beg
Rubha nan Totag Soay Mor
WEST LOCH
TARBERT
Taransay Teilesg
267
Ben Raah Beinn
Aird 5
Vanish Paible Luskent
Rubha
Sgeinigin Corran
Seilebost
Rubha
Romagi Seilebost
Toe Head 23 Clett Nisabost
Rubha Mas Heilisval Beg
Coppay a'Chnuic Borvemore
339 Bulaval 248 An Coi
Chaipeval SOUTH 354 384 386
368 Maodal 398 Braigh-nam-bagh
Shillay Traigh na Cleavag 251 Loch
Langavat HARRIS
Little Shillay Northton
Flodaba
Beinn a'Charnain
Ensay Mas
Pabbay 196 Garbh
Bailenacille Leverburgh Roneval Ardvey
Quinish Carminish 459
Islands
Caolas Strean Carminish 211
Rubh'a'Chorrain Rodel
Killegray Langay Rubha Vallarip
Berneray Massacamber Renish
Borve Point
86 Risgary Groay Gilsay
Haskeir Island Boreray Lingay
Haskeir Eagach Scaravay Narstay
Huilish Point Lingay Opsay
Veilish Point Newtonferry Hermetray
Valley Newton Aird
Griminish Point Goulaby Thormaid Loch
Scolpaig Oronsay 3 190 Aulasay
Balelone Middlequarter Sollas Trumisgarry Leac na Hoe
A865 12 B893 Scarts Rock
Manish Point Malaclete 171 Keallasay
Tigharry Balmartin Botarua Maari Crogan More
Loch Hosta Mor Keallasay
Hosta 180 Beg 5 Loch
Hougharry Portain
Aird NORTH UIST 5
Causamul an Runair Marrival Flad
Balranald 230 Loch Loch
Scadava Skellir Lochmaddy
Rubha 8 Loch Loch Madadh Beag
Port Scolpaig Huna Loch nan Eun
Bayhead Loch Madadh Mor
Paible a'Bharpa 8 North Lee
Balemore Deasker 251 Madadh Gruamach
Oitir Claddach
Mhor Kirkibost 280
Rubha Raouill Claddach
SOUND OF MONACH kyles A867 Loch An t-Aigeach
Huski Langass Hunera
Shillay Kirkibost Island Loch Eport Rubha Mhic
Monach Islands Gille-mhicheil
Hearnish Stockay B894 Loch Eigneig Mhor
Ceann Iar Teanamachar Samala Obisary
Ceann Ear Eaval Eigneig Bheag
Corunna 347 LITTL
Baleshare 9 Loch
Eachkamish Lavat MINCH
Carinish Floddaybeg
Oitir Mhor Floddaymore
Balaglas Bagh na Caiplich
Beul an Toim Grimsay 116
Flodday Ronay
Benbecula Gramisdale Kallin
Cnoc an t-seagail Uachdar 99
Aird Balivanich A865 Rubha na Rodagrich
Garry-a- Nunton Rueval Maragay Beg
siar 8 124 Maragay Mor
BENBECULA Loch Uskavagh
Griminish
Torlum Loch
Liniclett Olavat Uskavagh Maaey Riabhach
Hornish Point Creagorry B891 Rubha Cam nan Gail
Ardivachar Point Balgarva 4
Clachan 102 Wiay
Ardivachar Bagh nam Faoileann
DANGER ZONE Luirsay Dubh
Loch Gasay Luirsay Glas
Bee
Drimore Ben Tarbert 168
Crogarry B890 Loch Loch Skiport
Stilligarry Sheila

**A** **B** **C** **D** **E**

0 1 2 3 4 5  10  15 kilometres
0 1 2 3 4 5  10 miles

**A** **B** **C** **D** **E**

Beannan Mor 242
Loch Sheil
Eilean Iubhard
Srianach
Gob na Milaid

Corlabhadh
Loch nam Faoileag 371
Uisenis
Mulhagery

Crionaig 470

Tathas Mhor

SOUND OF THE MINCH

Bhlamus
Rubha Bhrollum
Rubh'a'Bhaird
Sgeir-na h-Eigheach
an Mor haigh

Garbh Eilean
Eilean Mhuire
161
Shiant Islands
Eilean an Tighe
Sgeir Mianish

SOUND OF SHIANT

Rubha Reidh
Camas Mor
Loch Draing
Sron Eilean an Air
An Cuaidh 296

Melvaig
Aultgrishan
293
Cnoc Bre
Peterburn
B8021
North Erradale 10

Fladda-chuain
Gaeilavore Island
Gearran Island
Eilean Trodday

Big Sand
B8021 St
Longa Island
Strat

GAIR LOCH

Rubha Hunish
Lub a Sgurhain
Rubha na h-Aiseig
Loch Hunish
Dun tulm B
The Aird
Kilmaluag Bay
Kilmaluag
Tulm Island
Duntulm A855 19
Galta Mor
Score Bay
Sgeir Eirin
Rubha Bornesketaig
Flodigarry
Eilean Flodigarry
Camas Mor

Port Henderson 9
Loch Clair
Opinan
South Erradale

Hunglader
Quirang
Staffin Island
Kilvaxter
Meall na Suiramach 543
The Needle
Staffin Bay
Balgown
Loch Sneosdal
Suidh' a'Mhinn 350
Stenscholl
Rubha Garbhaig
Monkstadt
Bioda Buidhe 464
Staffin
Linicro
Kilbride Point
Loch Cleap
Kilt Rock
Idrigil Uig
Ben Gorm
Maligar
L Mealt

Redpoint
Maol Ruadh
Red Point
Meall na Uamha 287
Sgeir na Trian
Craig

Stack of Skudiburgh
Sheader
Beinn Edra 611
Marishader
Garros
Rubha nam Brathairean
Culnaknock
Rubha Idrigill
Earlish
Creag Chragach
TROTTERNISH
Lealt

Eilean Iosal
Eilean Creagach
Ascrib Islands
South Ascrib
Rubha Chorachan
A856

LOCH SNIZORT
Stac a'Bhothain
Poll na h-Ealaidh
Creag a'Lain 608
Baca Ruadh 637
Leac Tressirnish
Port an Fhearainn

Rubha nam Fearn
Rubha na Fearn
Fearnmore
Fearnbeg
L Die

Biod nan Laogh
SNIZORT
Lyndale Point
Hinnisdal
Beinn a Sga
Rigg

Dry Harbour 125
RONA

Arinacrinachd
Cuaig
Loch a Chraoich
Kenmore

Ben Diubaig 214
Eilean Mor
Greshornish Point
Kingsburgh
Beinn a Sga 451
Hartaval
The Storr 719

Eilean Garbh
Abheinn Chuaig
Ardheslaig
Inverbain

Greshornish
Lyndale
Romesdal
Old Man of Storr
13
Eilean Tigh
Garbh-Eilean
An Garbh-mheall 492
Croic-bheinn
Lonbain
Loch Gaineamhach 493
Meall na Fhuaid 518

Beinn Chreagach
A886
A850
Arnisort
Treaslane
The Aird
Eyre
Lon Mor
Haultin
Kensaleyre
Beinn a'Chearcaill

Holm Island
Eilean Sguirr
Loch Arnish
An Dubh loch
626

Edinbain
Bernisdale
Totescore
Borve
Beinn a'Chearcaill 552
Loch Fada

Manish Point
Torran 254
Arnish

Ben Horneval 264
Ben Uigshader 246
Garbost
Skeabost
Drumuie
Ben Eassie 393

Prince Charles's Cave
Glame
Brochel

Applecross For
Carn Dearg
646

Ben Sca 265
Cruachan Beinn a'Chearcaill 271
Loch Ravag 208
Glengrasco
Rubha na h Airde Glaise
A850

SKYE
Loch Connan
Am Maol 212
Glenmore
Portree
Udairn
Balachuirn

Harlosh
Osdale
Beinn na Cloiche 230
Loch Duagrich
Ben Duagrich 304
Mugea
c-bheinn 396
Beinn Grasco
Beinn na Greine 417
Beinn Tianavaig 413
Glame 379
Sron na h-Airde Baine

Hartfield
Applecross
Milton
Camusteel
Camusterrach
Culduie
Loch Braigh an Achaidh
Meall Gor

Bracadale
Struan
Tarner Island
Mugea
Camashanavaig
Oskaig
Dun Caan 443
Rubha na' Leac
Toscaig

LOCH TORRIDON
SOUND OF RAASAY
INNER SOUND
SOUND OF RAASAY

A  B  C  D  E

**Summer Isles**
To Stornoway
Glas-leac Mor
Bol stol
Polbain
Achiltibuie
Am Blàr a'Chaill
Forest Stac Polly
612
Cul Beag 769
849
Drumrunie Forest
Elphin
Knockan
307
Cnoc na Glas Choille
Tanera Beg
Tanera Mor
489
601
Coigach
A835
Drumrunie
516
Cromalt Hills
578
Loch Craggie
Glas-leac Beag
Horse Island
743
Geodha Mor
Camas Mor
Horse Sound
Culnacraig
Strathkanaird
Strath
17
Kanaird
Na Dromannan
408
Strath nan Lon
Rappach
Meall an Fhuarain
Priest Island
Bottle Island
Carn nan Sgeir
Leac Dhonn
Isle Martin
Loch Cansird
Cul a'Bhogha
Rhue
Ardmair
29
Coire a'
578
Rhidorroch Forest
Rappach Water
Greenstone Point
Opinan
Rubha Mor
Leac Mhor
Rubha Beag
Cailleach Head
Stattic Point
Scoraig
Achmore
Annat Bay
Rhireavach
Morefield
Ullapool
Ullapool
Braes of Ullapool
Rhidorroch
Glen Achall
Loch Achall
Meall Liath Choire 548
Knockdamph
Loch an Daimh
Mellon Udrigle
Achgarve
Gruinard Island
GRUINARD BAY
Badluarach
Durnamuck
Beinn Ghobhlach 635
543
Cnoc a' Bhaid-rallaich
Allt na h'Airbhe
Beinn Eilideach 578
Leckmelm
Meall Dubh 642
Strath Mulzie
Corriemulzie
Laide
Coast
Mungasdale
A832
Badcaul
Badrallach
30
Loggie
Blarnalevoch
Rhiroy
Ardcharnich
Glen Douchary
Carn nam Bradhan 677
Freevater F
Mellon Charles
Ormiscaig
Bualnaluib
Aultbea
Little Gruinard
Carn na Beiste
300
Ardessie
Sail Mhor
Camusnagaul
Dundonnell
Eilean Darach
Ardindrean
Letters
Inverlael Forest
Carn Mor 647
a'Choire Mhoir
Seana Bhraigh 927
Isle of Ewe
Loch a'Bhaid luachraich
Carn nam Buailtean 391
Creag-mheall Beag 347
Gruinard Forest
Strathnasheallag Forest
Bidein a'Ghlas Thuill 1061
An Teallach
Sgurr Fiona 1059
Dundonnell Forest
Inverbroom
Auchlunachan
Glackour
Inverlael
Inverael
926
Meall nan Ceapraichean 977
Beinn Dearg 1081
Glenbeg
Boor
Poolewe
Londubh
INVEREWE (NTS)
Meall na Meine 250
680
Beinn a'Chaisgein Beag
Fisherfield Forest
Beinn a'Chaisgein Mor 854
Strath na Sealga
Auchindrean
Fasagrianach
Fain
Braemore
Carn Breac Beag
Dirrie More
Meall Leacachain 618
Beinn Enaiglair 889
Beinn Dearg 1081
347
Loch na Moine
Lochan Beannach 791
Beinn Airigh Charr
Dubh Loch
Beinn Dearg Mor 906
Beinn a'Chlaidheimh
Sgurr Ban 989
Meall an t-Sithe 601
A832
Creag Dhubh 522
Tom Ban Mor
Strathvaich Forest
Uchtercairn
Loch Airigh a' Phuill
Meall Mheannidh
A'Mhaighdean 960
Fuar Loch Mor
Mullach Coire Mhic Fhearchair
Creag Rainich 807
Abhainn
Meall a'Chrasgaidh 933
Beinn Liath Bheag 662
Loch Droma
A835
20
Beinn Liath Mhor a'Ghiubhais Li 751
Charlestown
Kerrysdale
Meall Aundrary
Eilean Ruairidh Mor
Eilean Subhainn
326
A832
Slattadale
Beinn Lair 859
Beinn Tarsuinn 930
Beinn Bheag
Groban 739
A'Chailleach 999
Sgurr Breac
Sgurr nan Clach Geala
Sgurr Mor 1109
Abhainn a'Ghiubhais Li
Meall Mhic Iomhair 605
Talladale
Furnace
Letterewe
Loch Garbhaig
18
Strath Lungard
Loch Maree
Sgurr nan Clach Geala
Meallan Chuaich
Fannich Forest
Loch Li
Loch Gorm
Kinlochluichart Forest
Beinn Dearg 680
Meall
Slioch 980
Gleann Bianasdail
Beinn a'Mhuinidh 680
Gleann na Muice
Cleann Tanagaidh
711
Beinn nan Ramh
Meall Gorm 948
An Coileachan 923
Carn na Beiste 512
Mullach nan Cadhaichean 293
Shieldaig Forest
Loch a'Ghobhainn
Baosbheinn 874
Beinn an Eoin 705
Ruadh-stac Mor 855
Meall a'Ghiubhais
Rhu Noa
Taagan
Kinlochewe Forest
Heights of Kinlochewe
Srath Chrombuill
Abhainn Bruachaig
Fannich
Lochrosque Forest
Carn Daraich 558
Loch Fannich
A832
16
Beinn Bhreac 619
Beinn Alligin 985
Beinn Dearg 921
Sail Mhor 981
Beinn Eighe
Kinlochewe
46
Glen Docherty
933
Fionn Bheinn
Meall a'Chaorainn 705
Knockban
Strath Bran
Brahan
Carn na Cre
Crea nan C
TORRIDON ESTATE (NTS)
Torridon Forest
Liathach 1024 1053
A896
Glen Torridon
A'Ghairbhe
Lubmore
A832
9
Badavanich
Achnasheen
Ledgowan Forest
Carn Chaiseachain 312
Sgurr a'Ghlas Leathaid 847
Milltown
Shuas
Inver Alligin
Faseg
Torridon
436
Seana Mheallan
Sgurr Dubh 782
Carn Loisgte
Loch an Fhiarlaid
An Liathanach
Glen Carron
Cnoc an t-Sidheim 371
Carn Mhartuin 538
Carn an Leanaid 561
Meallan nan Uan 867
Sgurr a'Mhuilinn
Balgy
Ben-damph Forest
Annat
735
Beinn na h-Eaglaise
Lochan Neimhe
Lochan Uaine
925
868
Beinn Liath Mhor
Carn Breac 678
Loch Sgamhain
Moruisg 928
Carn Liath 857
Meall na Faochaig 680
Scardroy
Carnoch
Inverchoran
Meall Giubhais 662
Glenmeanie
Ben Shieldaig 516
Maol Chean-dearg 933
Sgorr Ruadh 958
A890
Glen
Carron
18
Craig
55
Glencarron Forest
Carn Gorm 874
Glencarron Forest
Gleann Fhiodhaig
Bac an Eich 849
STRATHCONON
FOREST
shieldaig Forest
Beinn Damh 901
An Staonach 513
Meall na Saobhaidhe 368
An Ruadh-stac 890
Fuar Tholl 905
Balnacra
Achnashellach Forest
Sgurr nan Ceannaichean
Sgurr a'Chaorachain 1053
Maoile Lunndaidh 1007
Sgurr Coire nan Eun 787
Carn Eiteige 881
Sgurr na Muice 889
Carn na Gobhar 992
Sgurr na Ruaidhe 998
10
Coulags
Loch Dughaill
Loch Coultrie
Sgurr a Gharaidh 730
Glen Carron
Lair
Achnashellach
Creag a'Chaorainn Eagain
Bearnais
Beinn Tharsuinn
Sgurr a'Chaorachain
West Monar Forest
East Monar Forest
Loch Mhuilich
Sgurr a Choire Ghlais 1083
Sgurr na Cairbe
Carn Coinn
A896
8
Lochcarron
Attac
Achintee
Carn Geuradainn 594
Strathcarron Sta.
Uisge Dubh
986
An Gead Loch
Meallan Odhar Ilan Buidhe
Loch Monar
Bealach an Sgoltaidh
Loch Dughaill
An Gorm Loch
Loch Caoidhe
Abhainn
Gleann Strathfarrar

A  B  C  D  E

A B C D E

Crioc Leamhnachd
Aberscross
Kilbraur
Gordonbush
Col-bheinn 539
Lothbeg
394
Kilmote
Sron Rubha na Gaoithe
Lothbeg Point

Brora
Tannachy
Kilbraur Hill 324
Carrol Rock
Killin
Kintradwell

Rhilochan
Ben Horn 520
Carrol
Achrimsdale
West Clyne
Greenhill
Dalchalm

Blairmore
Rogart
Farlary
Loch Horn
Cagar Feosaig
Killin Rock
Clynelish
East Brora
Brora

Little Rogart
Pittentrail
Halt
Glen Rock
Glen
Beinn Lunndaidh
Backies
Doll

Morvich Lo.
Loch Lunndaidh 446
Beinn a' Bhragaidh
Rhives
35
9

Dalnamain
Aberscross
Mound Rock
Culmaily
DUNROBIN

Little Torboll
Kirkton
Golspie

Ardshave
Skelbo
Littleferry

Badninish
Skelbo
Badninish
Fourpenny
Embo

Achosnich
Birichen
Poles
Embo Street

Evelix
Proncy
Pitgrudy

Gablon
Clashmore Wood
Evelix
Dornoch

Clashmore
Lonemore
Dornoch Sands
Dornoch Firth

A9 SKIBO
Cuthill
Whiteness Sands
Innis Mhor
Tarbat Ness

Ardjachie Point
Port Mor
Wilkhaven

Morangie
Balcherry
Innis Bheag
Portmahomack
Bindal
Hilton

Tain
Inver
Rockfield

Morangie Forest
Balnagall
Tarrel

Knockbreck
Lochslin

Aldie
L. Eye
Baldie

Lamington
Newfield
Loandhu
Hill of Fearn
Rhynie
Geanies Ho.

Logie Hill
Calrossie
Fearn Sta.
Fearn
Cadboll

Balnagown Castle
Clays of Allan
Tullich
Hilton of Cadboll

ullich Muir
Milton
Ankerville
Balintore
Shandwick

Kilmuir
Tarbat Ho.
Chapelhill

Barbaraville
Delny
Nigg
Hill of Nigg

Balintraid
Saltburn
Sands of Nigg
Nigg Bay

nvergordon
Balnabruaich
Balnapaling
Castlecraig
North Sutor

Dunskeath Ness
Cromarty
Sutors Stacks

HUGH MILLER'S COTTAGE
Blue Head
McFarquhar's Cave

Shoremill
Newton
Navity

Muirton
Upper Eathie
Craighead

Glenurquhart

Balmungie
Janefield
Whiteness Head

emarkie Bay
Rosemarkie
Fort George
Carse of Ardersier
Hilton of Delnies
Kingsteps
Macbeth's Hillock

Fortrose
Chanonry Point
Ardersier
Kirkton
Nairn
Dyke
Brodie
Forres
SUENO'S STONE

Findhorn
Culbin Forest
Binsness
Findhorn Bay
Kincorth House
Moy
Invererne
Grange Hall
Springfield

Covesea Skerries
Stotfield
Covesea
Clashach Point
Burghead
Hopeman
Gordonstoun
Duffus
Roseisle

Cummingston
Burghead Bay
Roseisle Forest
DUFFUS
Findrassie

Elgin
Buthill
Quarrywood
Crook of Alves
Pittendreich
Miltonduff
New Elgin
Palmersc

The Bar
Kintessack
Tradespark
Househill
Darnaway
Califer
Rafford
Tulloch
Westerton
Barnhill
Auchtertyre
Thoms

Moss-side
Auldearn 1645
Boghole
Whitemire
Mains of Burgie
Heldon Hill
PLUSCARDEN
Cloddach

Blackcastle
Laiken Forest
Conicavel
Milton
Mains of Sluie
Briach
Dallas
Craigend
Glenlatterach

Gollanfield
Muir of the Clans
Brackley
Torrich
Righoul
Darnaway Forest
Phorp
Branchill
Edinvale
Hill of the Wangie

Fisherton
Inverness (Dalcross)
Drumine
Clephanton
Cawdor
Piperhill
Culcharry
Littlemill
Fornighty
Lethen Bar
Logie
Presley
Tomnamoon
Romach Hill
Ardoch
Pikey Hill

Tornagrain
Newton
Dalcross
Croy
Dallaschyle
CAWDOR
Urchany
Shaw Hill
Relugas
Hill of Tomechole
Meikle Hill
Cairn Uish

Cantraywood
Easter Galcantray
Achindown
Clunas
Redburn
Craigroy

Balloch
Culloden Forest
Cantray
Kirkton of Barevan
Bruachmary
Mount Ferness
Tomdow

Culloden Muir
Cantraydoune
Carn Maol
Balmore
Carn a'Chrasgie

Leanach
Dalroy
Assich Forest
Saddle Hill
Carn Sgumain Carnoch
Daltra
Dulsie
Milltown
Loch Dallas
Carnachie
Priestfield
Upper Knockando
Cardow

Castletown
Beinn Bhuidhe Mhor 548
Carn nan tri-tigheam 614
Daless
Banchor
Aitnoch of Aitnoch
Dava
Knock of Braemoray
Larig Hill
Cairn
Knockando
Carron

1 2 3 4 5 6 7

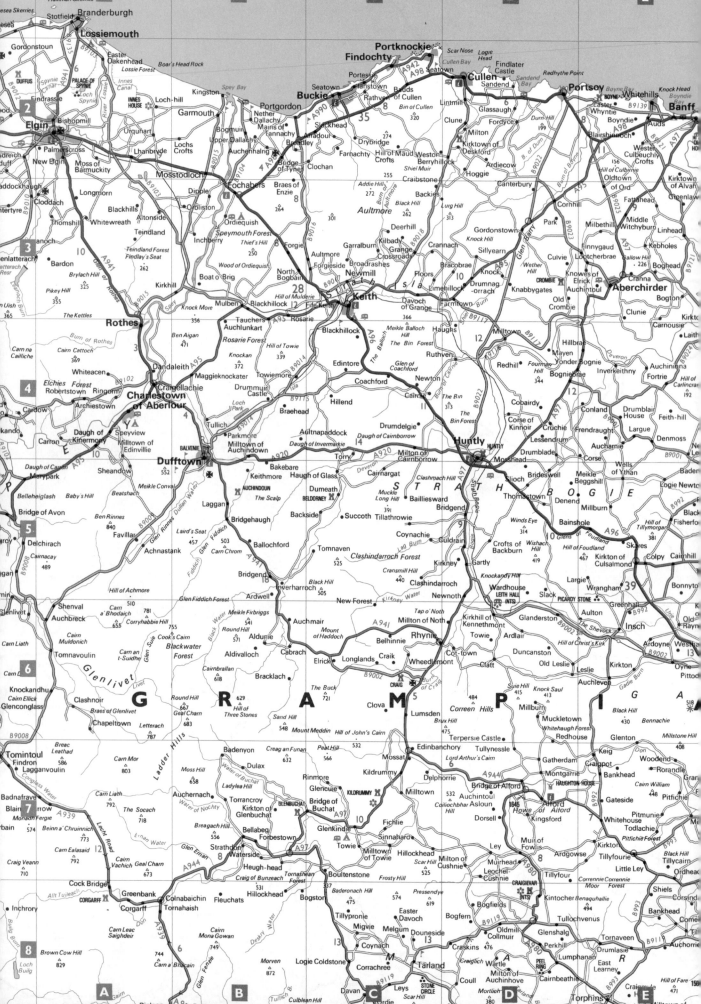

| 102 | 103 |
|---|---|
| 94 | 95 |

| 104 | 105 |
|---|---|
| 96 | 97 |

**A**  **B**  **C**  **D**  **E**

**Roseheary** Sandhaven Broadsea Kinnaird Head
**Fraserburgh**
Troup Head Northfield Pennan Head Quarry Head Peathill Pitsligo Pitblae Cairnbulg Point Cairnbulg
Crovie Head Gamrie Bay Crovie Pennan Coburty Cardno Broomhead Inverallochy
**cduff** Head of Garness **Gardenstown** Towie Mid Ardlaw Memsie Charlestown St Combs
Melrose Greenskairs Dubford Gamrie New Aberdour Upper Boyndlie Whitewell BURIAL CAIRN Cairness Inzie Head South Inch
Longmanhill Cushnie Lemnas Ladysford Rathen Craigellie Crofts of Savoch Seatown Rattray Head
Foulzie Minnonie Netherbrae Nether Glasslaw Whitebog Newburgh Crimongate Coralhill Strathbeg Bay
Balgreen Bracklamore Hill Craigmaud Hillhead of Auchentumb Dartfield Loch of Strathbeg Old Rattray
Gorrachie Bogfold Waughton Hill Crimond Blackhill Rattray Bay
Woodhead Bracklamore Turclossie Mormond Hill Logie North Essie
Milltown of Craigston New Pitsligo Knowhead Whitestripe New Leeds Upper Ridinghill Gas Terminal
Plaidy CRAIGSTON South Cowbog Brunthill Strichen Longhill Backfolds St Fergus
Fintry New Byth Craigculter Leys Denhead St Fergus Moss Scotstown Head
Brackens Bonnykelly Ironside Carnichal Fetterangus Rora Moss Kirkton Kirkton Head
Wester Badentyre Muiryfold Balthangie Oldwhat Forest of Deer Toux Hythie Cuttyhill Rora Lunderton
**Turriff** DELGATIE Cairncake Fedderate Waterhill of Bruxie Dunshillock Pitfour Millbank Craig Ewen
Cuminestown Delgaty Idoch Forest Middlehill Culsh Maud Old Deer Mintlaw Longside Torterston Inverugie **Peterhead**
Howe of Teuchar Northburnhill Grainhow New Deer Drum Drymuir Bulwark Aden Flushing Buchanhaven Keith Inch
Gask Ho. Darra Hatton Castle Waggle Hill Clockhill Nethermuir Stuartfield Millbreck Inverquhomery Thunderton Peterhead Bay
Birkenhills South Redbriggs Maryhill Tillyfar Crichie Clola Nether Kinmundy Little Burnhaven Invernettie
TOWIE BARCLAY Deer's Hill Kirkton Newmill Kinnadie Skelmuir Newton Dens Hillhead of Cocklaw Sandford Bay
Steinmanhill Darnabo Lethenty Knaven Smallburn Blackhill Buchan Ness
Inverythan Gourdas Monkshill Burnend Cairnorrie Upper Barrack Auchnagatt Skelmuir Hill Kinknockie Sandfordhill Boddam
Tifty Cot-town Brownhill Hill of Skilmafilly Elrick Mill Inkhorn Corse of Balloch Aldie
Backhill Woodhead Crofts of Haddo Ardo Monteach Skelmonae Loanhead Hawkhillock Greenheads Teuchan Coldwells
Fyvie Methlick Quilquox Arnage Milton Coldwells Gask Bullers of Buchan
Petty Flobbets St Katherines Greenmyre Collynie Drumwhindle Arthrath Dudwick Muirtack **Hatton** Auchiries Cruden Bay Errollston Slains
Folla Rule The Banking Barthol Chapel Earlsford Craigie Shethin Inverebrie Blindburn Hilton Bearnie Waterloo Bogbrae Chapel Hill Port Erroll Bay of Cruden
Cross of Jackson Balgove South Blackbog Wedderlairs Raxton Cookston Broomfield Artrochie Leask Kiplaw Croft The Skares Whinnyfold
Jackstown Tarves Kinharrachie **Ellon** Auchmacoy Clochtow The Veshels
Pitinnan Tulloch Craigdam Ythsie Meikle Loch Kirkton of Slains Collieston St Catherine's Dub
Mounie Castle Auquhorthies Toluhoun Esslemont Kirkton of Logie Buchan Forvie Ness or Hackley Head
**Oldmeldrum** Cairnbrogie Pitmedden Cairnhill Tippert Meikle Tarty Waterside Sands of Forvie
Fingask Hill of Barra Udny Green Old Craig Kinknockie Newburgh
Milton of Inveramsay Kingoodie Pittrichie Affleck Pettymuick Udny Station Kincraig Newburgh Bar
Balhalgardy Kirkton of Bourtie Hattoncrook Tillygreig Cultercullen Milltown of Minnes Foveran
**Inverurie** Hillbrae Whiteashes Tillycorthie Tillery Blairythan Drums Delfrigs Menie
Nether Crimond Whitlam Craigie Causeynd Orrok Ho.
Port Elphinstone Kinmuck Middleton Newmachar Blackbrass Whitecairns Balmedie BALMEDIE
**Kintore** Denmill Straloch Kinmundy Longdrum Belhelvie
Balbithan Wester Fintry Hatton of Fintray Cothal Millown Millden
Cottown Denhead Kinellar Tyrebagger Hill Skelly Rock
Leschangie Leylodge Overton Blackdog Blackdog Rock
Craigearn Burnside Blackburn Stoneywood Middleton Park Upper Tarbothill
Lauchintilly Blackchambers Clinterty Craibstone **Dyce** Mundurno Cloverhill
Lyne of Skene Tertowie Bankhead Danestone
Dunecht Kirkton of Skene Buxburn **Bridge of Don**
Brimmond Hill Old Aberdeen
Loch of Skene Northfield Fairley Woodside
Echt Westhill Kingswells Masthick **ABERDEEN**
Redhill Garlogie Elrick Kingsford Hazlehead Girdle Ness
Cullerlie Wester Ord Easter Ord Blacktop **Cults** Torry Nigg Bay Greg Ness
Kincorth Nigg
Banchory Souter Head
Cove Bay

**2 3 4 5 6 7 8**

To Stronsness To Lerwick

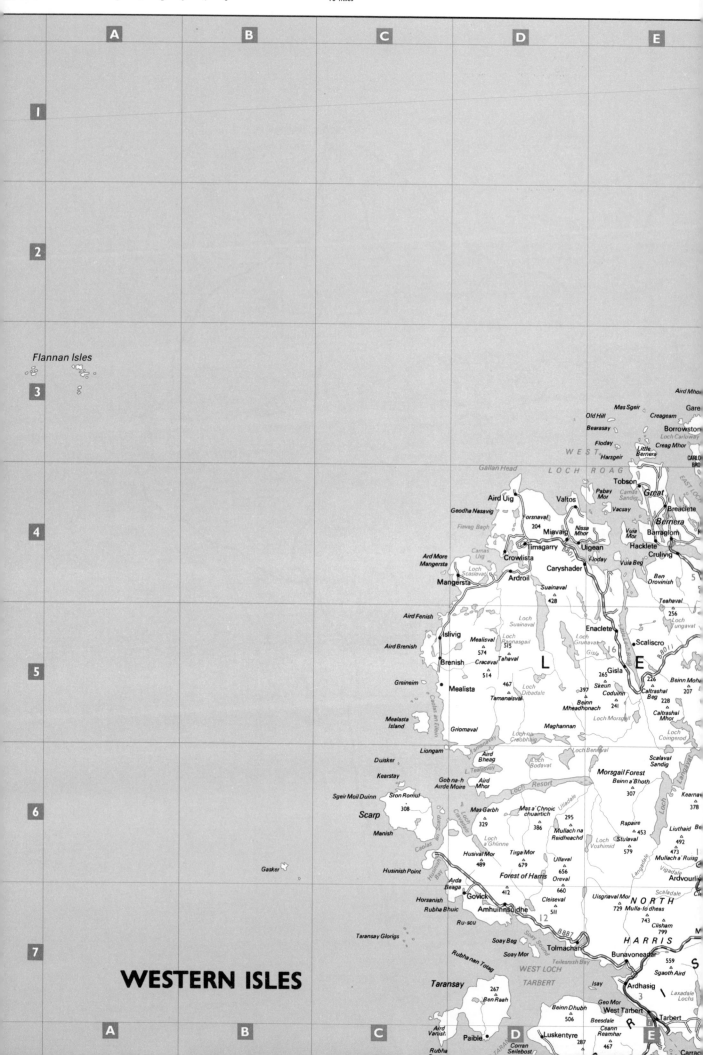

A B C D E

1

2

Flannan Isles

3

Aird Mhor
Mas Sgeir   Creageam   Gare
Old Hill   Borrowston
Bearasay   Loch Carloway
Floday   Creag Mhor
Harsgeir   Little   CARLO
Bernera   BRO
W E S T
GallanHead   LOCH ROAG   EAST LOCH

Tobson   Great
Pabay   Camas
Aird Uig   Valtos   Mor   Sandig
Geodha Nasavig   Forsnaval   Vacsay   Breaclete
Fianag Bagh   204   Nissa   Vuia   Bernera
4   Miavaig   Mhor   Mor   Barraglom
Ard More   Camas   Timsgarry   Uigean   Hacklete
Mangersta   Uig   Crowlista   Floday   Crulivig
Loch   Caryshader   Vuia Beg
Scaslavat   Ardroil   Ben
Mangersta   Drovinish
Suainaval   Teahaval
428   256
Aird Fenish   Loch   Loch
Suainaval   Enaclete   Tungavat
Islivig   Mealisval   Loch   Scaliscro
Aird Brenish   574   515   Loch   Gisla
Greineim   Brenish   Cracaval   Tahaval   Grunavat   6
5   514   Gisla   Gisla
Mealista   467   Loch   265   226   Beinn Mho
Tamanaisval   Dibadale   Skeun   Caltrashal   207
397   Coduinn   Beg   228
Mealasta   Beinn   241   Caltrashal
Island   Mheadhonach   Mhor
Griomaval   Maghannan   Loch Morsgail   Loch
Loch na   Coingerod
Liongam   Creobhaig   Loch Benaval
Aird   Scalaval
Duisker   Bheag   Loch   Sandig
Kearstay   L. Tealasvay   Bodavat   Morsgail Forest
Gob na-h   Aird   Beinn a'Bhoth
Sgeir Moil Duinn   Sron Romul   Airde Moire   Mhor   307   Kearna
6   308   Mas Garbh   Mas a'Chnoic   295   Rapaire
Scarp   329   chuairtich   453   Liuthaid Be
Manish   386   Mullach na   Stulaval   492
Loch   Reidheachd   Loch   579   Mullach a'Ruisg
a'Ghlinne   Voshimid
Husivat Mor   Tirga Mor   473
Husinish Point   489   679   Ullaval   656   Ardvourli
Arda   Forest of Harris   Oreval
Beaga   Govick   412   660   Scaladale
Horsanish   Cleiseval   Uisgnaval Mor   NORTH   Cle
Rubha Bhuic   Amhuinnsuidhe   511   729   Mulla-fo dheas
Ru-scu   743
12   Clisham   M
Taransay Glorigs   799
7   HARRIS
Rubha nan Totag   Soay Beg   Tolmachan   559
Soay Mor   Bunavoneadar   Sgaoth Aird
Teilesnish Bay   I S
WEST LOCH   Isay   Ardhasig   Laxadale
TARBERT   Geo Mor   3   Lochs
Taransay   267   Beinn Dhubh   West Tarbert
Ben Raah   506   Beesdale   R   Tarbert
Ceann   West Tarbert
Aird   Reamhar
Varnish   Luskentyre   L
Paible   Corran   287   Carrac
Rubha   Seilebost   467

**WESTERN ISLES**

A B C D E

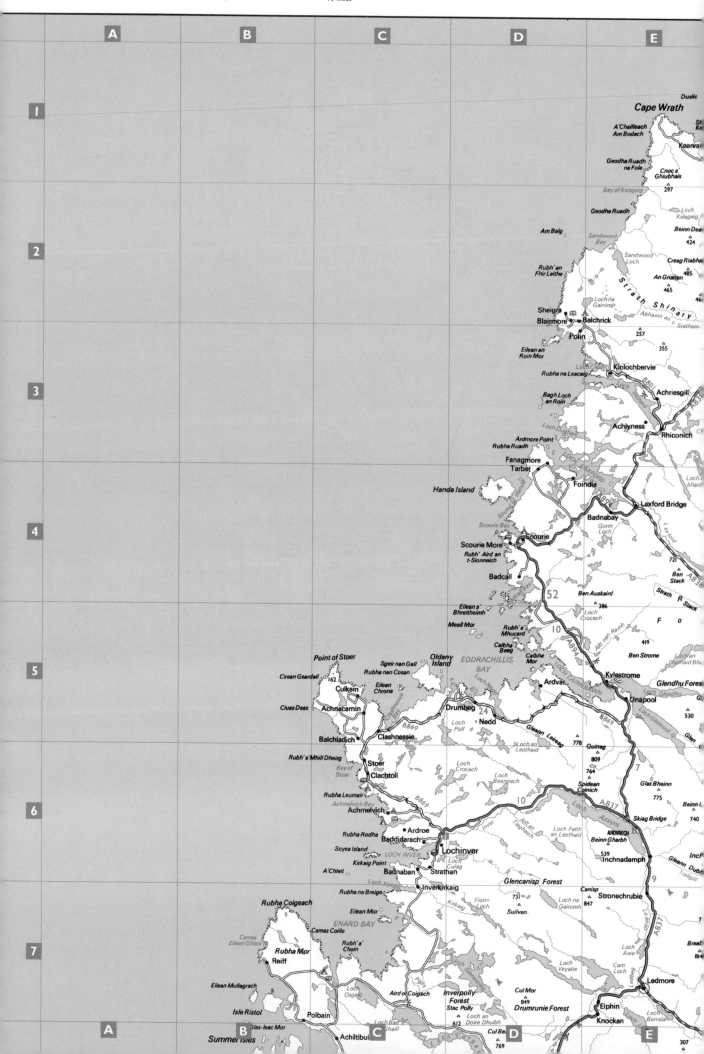

0 1 2 3 4 5      10       15 kilometres
0 1   2   3   4   5        10 miles

A     B     C     D     E

Duslic
Cape Wrath
A'Chailleach
Am Bodach
St
Ke
Kearvai

Geodha Ruadh
na Fola
Cnoc a
Ghiubhais
297

Bay of Keisgaig

Geodha Ruadh

Am Balg
Sandwood
Bay
Loch
Keisgaig

Beinn Dea
424

Sandwood
Loch
Creag Riabha

Rubh' an
Fhir Leithe
An Grianan
465
46

Loch na
Gainimh
Strath Shinary
Abhainn an t-Srathain

Sheigra
Blairmore
Balchrick
257

Polin
355

Eilean an
Roin Mor
Loch Clash
Kinlochbervie

Rubha na Leacaig
Achriesgill

Bagh Loch
an Roin
Loch Inchard

Ardmore Point
Rubha Ruadh
Achlyness
Rhiconich

Fanagmore
Tarbet
Loch Laxford
Loch
bhaid

Foindle

Handa Island
Laxford Bridge

Badnabay
Sound of Handa
Gorm
Loch

Scourie Bay
Scourie
7
Laxford

Scourie More
721

Rubh' Aird an
t-Sionnaich
Ben
Stack
A836

Badcall
52
Strath R Stack

Eilean a'
Bhreitheimh
Ben Auskaird
386
F o

Meall Mor
Loch
Crocach
419

Rubh' a'
Mhucard
10

Calbha
Beag
Ben Strome

Point of Stoer
Sgeir nan Gall
Rubha nan Cosan
Oldany
Island
EDDRACHILLIS
BAY
Calbha
Mor
Loch
Leathaid Bh

Cirean Geardail
162
Eilean
Chrona
Loch Nedd
Kylestrome
Glendhu Fores

Culkein
Ardvar
Loch Glencoul
Unapool
Glen

Clus Deas
Achnacarnin
Drumbeg
24
Gleann Leiraig
778
Quinag
809
530

Balchladich
B869
Clashnessie
Loch
Poll
Nedd
Loch an
Leothaid
7

Rubh' a' Mhill Dheirg
Stoer
Clachtoll
Loch
Crocach
Loch
Beannach
764
Glas Bheinn
775

Bay of
Stoer
B869
Spidean
Coinich
Beinn L

Rubha Leumair
Achmelvich Bay
Achmelvich
B869
10
Loch
Assynt
A837
Skiag Bridge
740

Ardroe
Baddidarach
Inver
Allt an
Tiaghaich
ARDVRECH
Beinn Gharbh

Rubha Rodha
Loch Feith
an Leothaid
539
Inchnadamph

Soyea Island
Lochinver
Loch INVER
Incl
Gleann Dubh
Traligill

A'Chleit
Badnaban
Strathan
Loch
Culag
Glencanisp Forest
9

Kirkaig Point
Inverkirkaig
731
Canisp
847
Stronechrubie

Rubha na Breige
Kirkaig
Fionn
Loch
Loch na
Gainimh
A837

Rubha Coigeach
Eilean Mor
Suilven
Loch
Awe
Brea
814

ENARD BAY
Camas Coille

Camas
Eilean Ghlais
Rubh' a'
Choin
Loch
Veyatie
Cam
Loch

Rubha Mor
Reiff
Ledmore

Eilean Mullagrach
Inverpolly
Forest
Stac Polly
Cul Mor
849
Drumrunie Forest
Loch
Borralan

Isle Ristol
Loch
Osgaig
Aird of Coigach
Loch an
Doire Dhuibh
612
Elphin

Glas-leac Mor
Summer Isles
Achiltibuie
Cul Be
769
Knockan
307

A     B     C     D     E

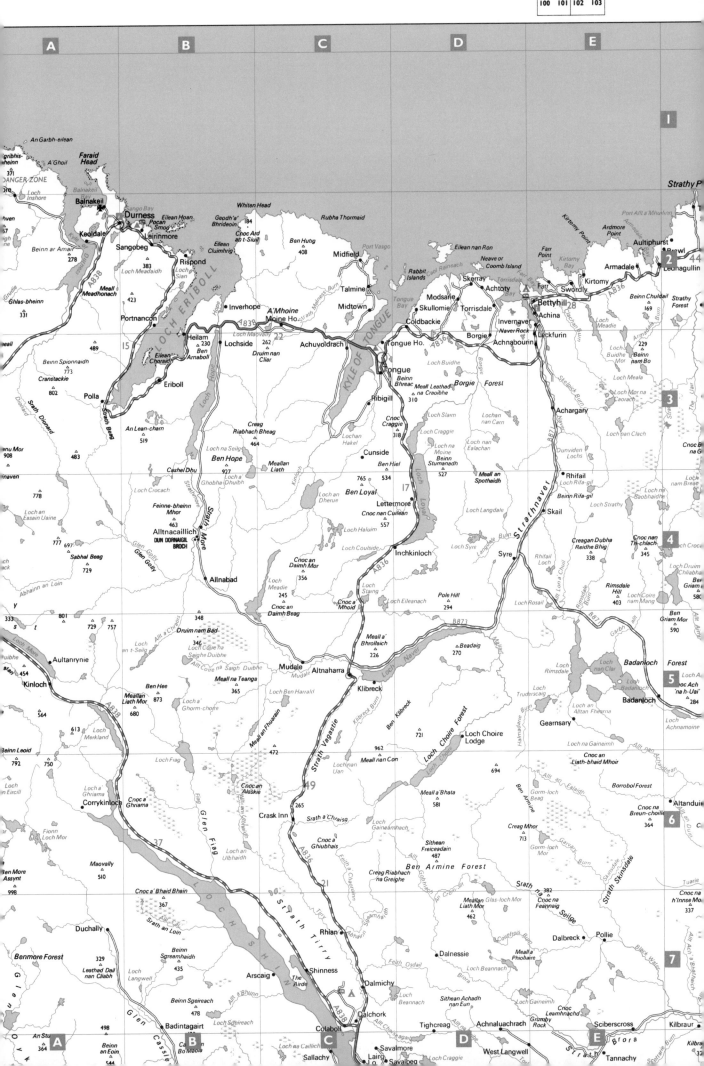

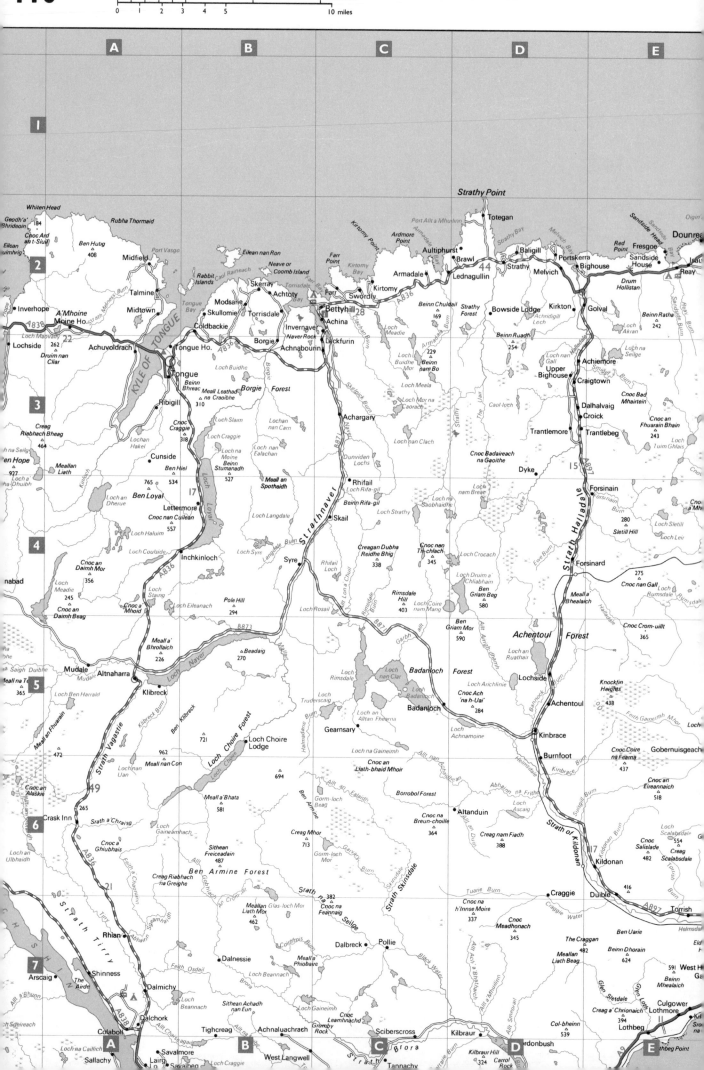

Pentland Firth

**Dunnet Head**

Langaton Point
Island of Stroma
Red Head
Nethertown
Uppertown

Muckle Skerry
Pentland Skerries

To Stromness

Easter Head
Burifa Hill
Little Cliett
The Stacks
Scarfskerry Point
Tang Head
St John's Point
Men of Mey
Mell Head
Head of Crees
Boars of Duncansby
Ness of Duncansby
Ness of Sannick
Duncansby Head
To Burwick (Proposed)
Inner Sound

Briga Head
121
Dunnet Hill
Red Geo
Brough
Ham
Scarfskerry
Harrow
East Mey
CASTLE OF MEY
Gills
John o'Groats
Stacks of Duncansby

Grim's Ness
Port of Brims
Ness of Litter
Spear Head
Cliett
Holborn Head
The Thirl
Hunspow
Rattar
Whitebridge
Mey
St John's Loch
Loch of Mey
Gills Bay
Huna
Upper Gills
A836
Canisbay
Warth Hill
Hill of Crogodale
124

Dwarwick Head
The Spur
Clardon Head
DUNNET
Dunnet
Links of Dunnet
Barrock
Inkstack
Brabster
Tofts
Freswick
Everley
Skirza
Skirza Head
Freswick Bay

Crosskirk
Scrabster
THURSO BAY
Muckle Bay
BAY
Greenland
Lochend
Slickly
Upper Gills
Warth
Ness Head

Thurso
Clardon
Stitley
Haimer
Murkle
Castletown
Thurdistoft
Tain
Lochside
Reaster
Slickly
Alterwall
Auckingills
Nybster

Lybster
Bridge of Forss
Viewfield
Ormelie
Olrig House
Hayfield
Lochside
Bowermadden
Lyth
Sortat
Howe
Keiss
Stain
Brough Head

Achreamie
Lythmore
Janetstown
Newlands of Geise
Glengolly
Shalmstry
Weydale
Carsgoe
Achingills
Hoy
Bowertower
17

Shebster
Forsie
Westfield
Buckies
Lieurary
Aimster
Skinnet
Braal Castle
Sordale
Knockdee
Stemster
Tister
Corsback
Halcro
Hastigrow
Mireland
Tang Head

Broubster
Loch Calder
Calder Mains
Gerston
Georgemas Junc. Sta.
Clayock
Stemster House
Gillock
North Watten
Kirk
Loch of Wester
Keiss
Stain

Halkirk
Shurrery
Brawlbin
Scotscalder Sta.
Bloody Moss
Harpsdale
Achies
Dunn
Old Hall
21
Watten
Mains of Watten
Whitefield
Loch of Winless
SINCLAIRS BAY

Shurrery Lodge
Loch Shurrery
Ben Dorrery
244
Dorrery
Olgrinmore
Spittal Hill
Houstry of Dunn
Newton
Backlass
15
Winless
Reiss
Sibster
Quoys of Reiss

Blair Dearg
Westerdale
Mybster
Loch of Toftingall
Bilbster
Strath
Thuster
Haster
SINCLAIR
ACKERGILL TOWER
Ackergill
Noss Head
GIRNIGOE
Staxigoe

Tormsdale
Kensary
Badlipster
Stirkoke House
Milton
Newton
Wick
Broad Haven
North Head
Wick Bay
Sealky Head

Tacher
Stemster
Hill of Rangag
145
Ballharn Hill
Lower Camster
GREY CAIRNS
Loch of Yarrows
Puldagon
Tannach
Northfield
Whiterow
OLD WICK
South Head
Gote o' Tram

Achscoriclate
Balavreed
Coire na Beinne
226
Stemster Hill
248
Cnoc an Earrannaiche
Hill of Yarrows
213
17
Hempriggs House
Helman Head
Ires Geo
Toftcarl
Thrumster
Corbiegoe
Sarclet
Sarclet Head

Beinn Chaiteag
Loch Ruard
Lochan Thulachan
Loch Sand
Upper Camster
CAIRN OF GET
Whaligoe
Whiteleen
Ulbster
Stack of Ulbster
Ellen's Geo

Sheppardstown
Roster
East Clyth
Bruan
Crofts of Benachielt
Ben-a-chielt
Rumster Forest
Upper Lybster
37
Upper Clyth
STONE ROWS
Mid Clyth
Blackness
Halberry Head
Clyth Ness

Ben-Alisky
349
Loch Breac
Loch Dubh
Cnocan Conachreag
268
43
Nottingham
Houstry
Reisgill
Swiney
Lybster
Occumster

Cnoc na Gaobhaidhe
290
Achnaclyth
Pollroy
Gillivoan
Forse
Smerral
Latheron
Janetstown

Dunbeath Water
Badnagie
Achorn
Toremore
Inver
Dunbeath
Dunbeath Bay

Braemore
Knockally
Ramscraigs

Maiden Pap
484
Scaraben
626
Meall na Caorach
Borgue
An Dun
Newport
20

Wag
Langwell Forest
Mid Hill
313
Aultibea
Langwell Water
Langwell House
Berriedale
Cnoc na Croiche
Braigh na h-Eaglaise
423
Boch-ailean

A9
Ousdale
Badbea

Creag Thoraraidh
Caen
Ord of Caithness
Navidale
East Helmsdale
Helmsdale
Portgower

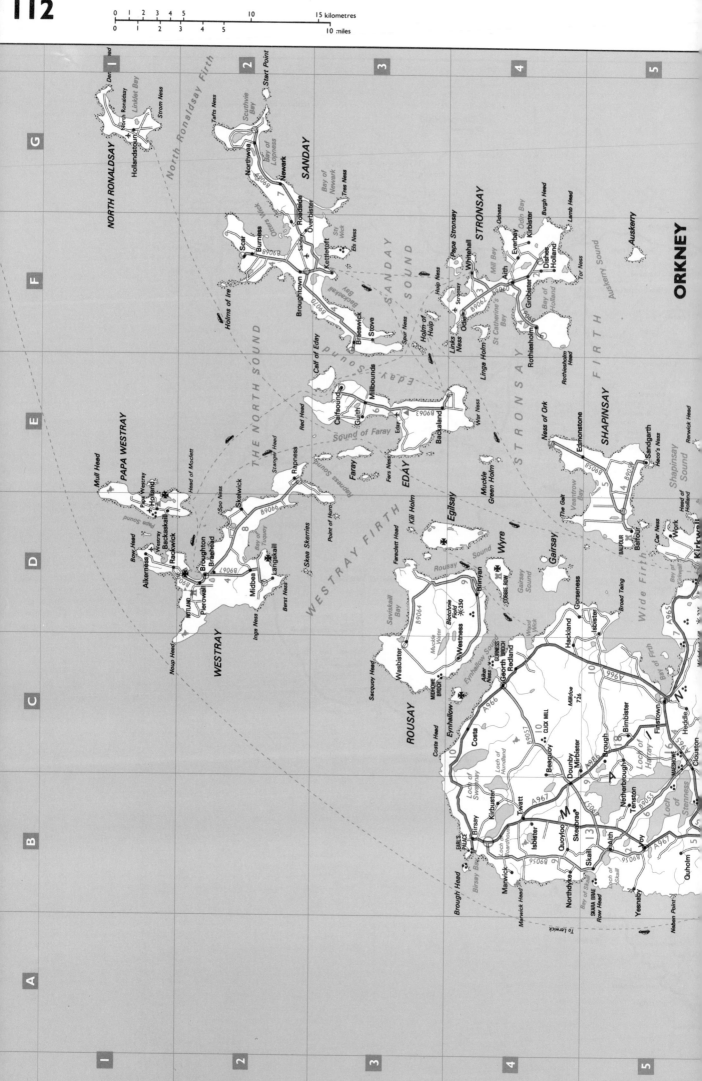

0 1 2 3 4 5          10          15 kilometres
0 1    2    3    4    5          10 miles

**ORKNEY**

NORTH RONALDSAY

Den Head
North Ronaldsay
Linklet Bay
Strom Ness
Hollandstoun

North Ronaldsay Firth

Start Point
Tafts Ness
Scuthvie Bay
Northwaa
SANDAY
Bay of Lopness
Newark
Roadside
Overbister
Bay of Newark
Tres Ness
Otters Wick
Burness
Scar
Kettletoft
Sty Wick
Els Ness
Broughtown
Backaskaill Bay
Braeswick
Stove
Holms of Ire

SANDAY SOUND

Spur Ness
Huip Ness
Holm of Huip

STRONSAY
Papa Stronsay
Whitehall
Odness
Burgh Head
Lamb Head
Eversay
Kirbister
Dishes
Holland
Aith
Grobister
Bay of Holland
Odin Bay
St Catherine's Bay
Links Ness
Odie
Rothiesholm
Rothiesholm Head
Tor Ness

AUSKERRY SOUND

Auskerry

THE NORTH SOUND

Holms of Ire

EDAY SOUND

Calf of Eday
Red Head
Stenger Head
Rapness
Skelwick
Calfsound
Guith
Millbounds
Backaland
B9063
Vinr Ness
Linga Holm

Sound of Faray

PAPA WESTRAY
Mull Head
Head of Moclett
Papa Westray
Holland
Bow Head
Backaskaill
Rackwick
Aikerness
MAITLAND
Pierowall
Broughton
Braehead
Midbea
Langskaill
WESTRAY
Spo Ness
Skea Skerries
Tuquoy
Berst Ness
Inga Ness
Noup Head
Papa Sound
Fers Ness
Faray
Point of Huro
Rapness Sound

EDAY
Muckle Green Holm
Kili Holm
Egilsay
Ness of Ork

SHAPINSAY
Edmonstone
Sandgarth
Haco's Ness
Veantrow Bay
The Galt
BALFOUR
Balfour
Car Ness
Work
Head of Holland
Berwick Head

WESTRAY FIRTH

Saviskaill Bay
Faraclett Head
Rousay Sound
ROUSAY
Wyre
DOBBIE ROW
Brinyan
Gairsay
Gairsay Sound
Wide Firth
Bay of Firth

Sacquoy Head
Costa Head
Eynhallow
Muckle Water
Wasbister
Westness
MIDHOWE BROCH
Blotchnie Field 250
B9064
Eynhallow Sound
Aiker Ness
GURNESS
GEORTH BROCH
Redland
Hackland
Isbister
Gorseness
Broad Taing

Costa
A966
CLICK MILL
Dounby
Mirbister
Beaquoy
Loch of Hundland
Loch of Swannay
Brough
Netherbrough
Tenston
Hilltoe 716
Millhoe
Bimbister
Firstown
Heddle
Clouston
Loch of Harray

EARL'S PALACE
Birsay
Kirbuster
Twatt
A967
Isbister
Quoyloo
Skeabrae
13
Skaill
Faith
A967
Voy
B9055
Loch of Stenness

Brough Head
Birsay Bay
Marwick
Marwick Head
Northdyke
SKARA BRAE
Row Head
Bay of Skaill
Loch of Skaill
Yesnaby
Neban Point
Quholm

To Lerwick

KIRKWALL
A965
MAESHOWE

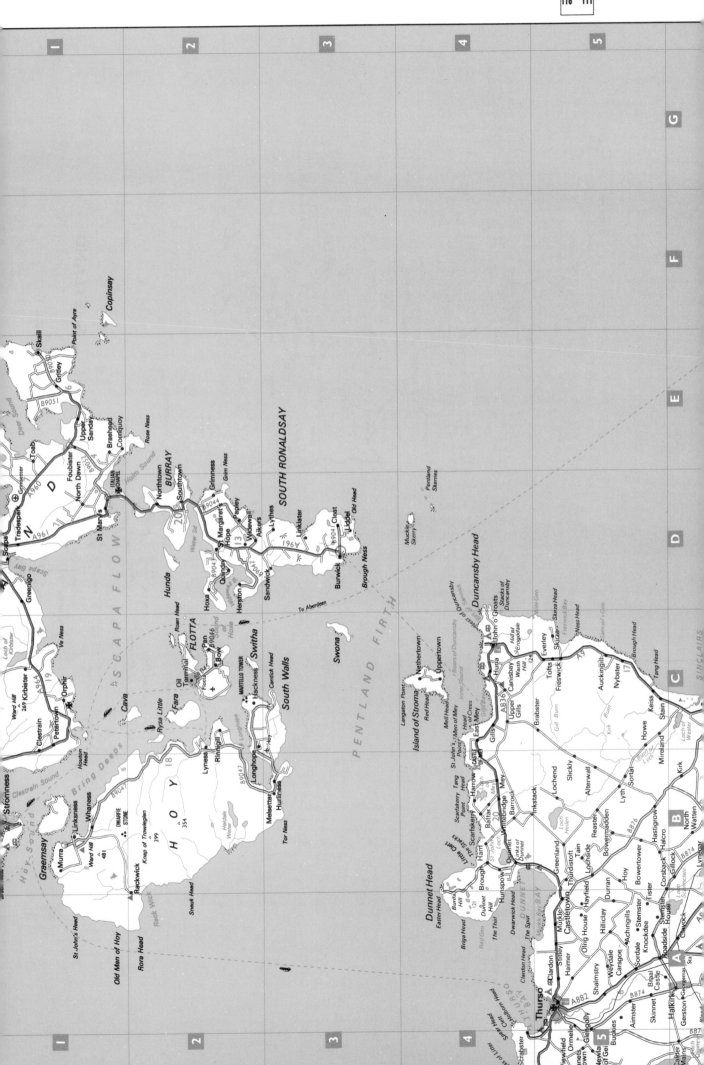

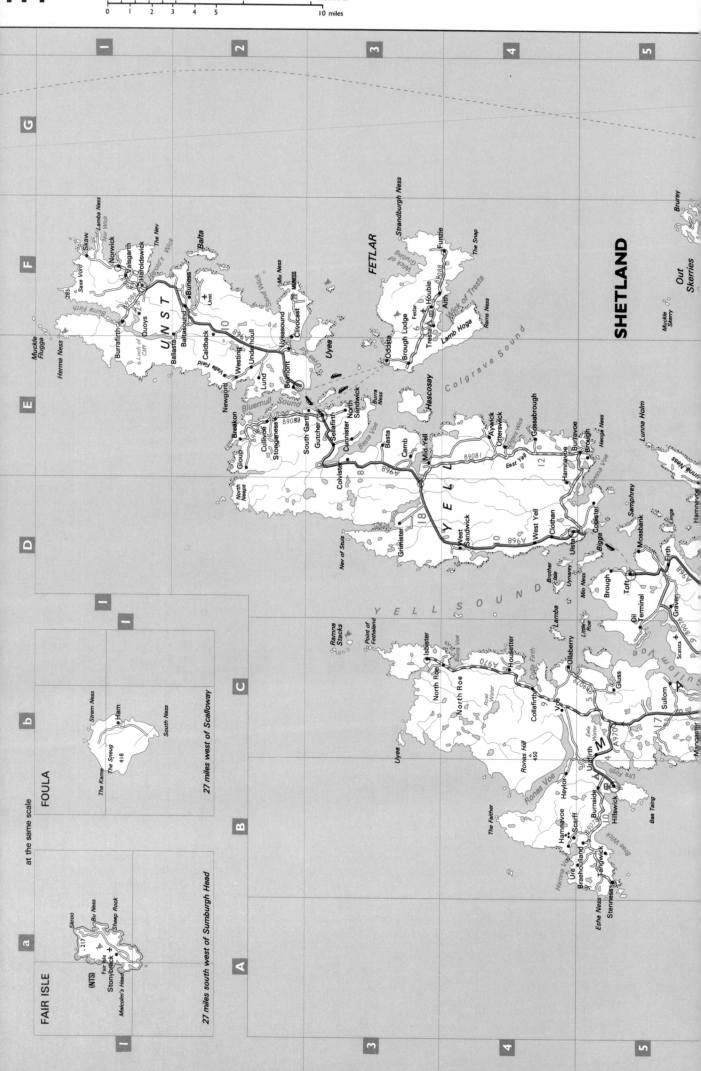

0 1 2 3 4 5    10    15 kilometres
0 1 2 3 4 5    10 miles

G 1    2    3    4    5

FAIR ISLE

at the same scale

FOULA

Strem Ness
Ham
The Kame
The Sneug
418
South Ness

27 miles west of Scalloway

Skroo
Bu Ness
217
Sheep Rock
Fair Isle
Stonybreck
Malcolm's Head
(NTS)

27 miles south west of Sumburgh Head

a    b    C    B    A

Muckle Flugga
Herma Ness
Burrafirth
Quoys
Skaw
Saxa Vord
Lamba Ness
Nor Wick
Norwick
Valsgarth
Haroldswick
The New
Sand Wick
Balta
Buness
Muness
UNST
Ballasta
Baltasound
Caldback
Valla Field
Westing
Underhoull
Sand Wick
Mu Ness
Vinetorne
Clivocast
Uyeasound
Muness
Unst
Newgord
Lund
Belmont
Uyea
Breakon
Bluemull Sound
Gloup
Cullivoe
Stonganess
South Garth
Gutcher
Sellafirth
Cunnister
North Sandwick
Basta Voe
Bura Ness

FETLAR
Strandburgh Ness
Wick of Gruting
Funzie
The Snap
Brough Lodge
Fetlar
Houbie
Tresta
Aith
Lamb Hoga
Rams Ness
Wick of Tresta

North Neeps
New of Stuis
Grimister
8
A968
18
YELL
Camb
Mid-Yell
East Yell
12
B9081
Aywick
Otterswick
Gossabrough
Colgrave Sound
Hascosay
Gutcher Wick

SHETLAND

Out Skerries
Bruray
Muckle Skerry

West Sandwick
West Yell
Clothan
Ulsta
A968
0
Copister
Bigga
Brough
Burravoe
Hannavoe
Brough
Heoga Ness
Hamna Voe
Samphrey
Mossbank
Lunna Holm
Lunna Ness
Linga
Hamnavoe

YELL SOUND
Brother Isle
Uynarea
Mio Ness
Lamba
Little Roe
Oil Terminal
Toft
Brough
Graven
Firth
A968
Scatsta
Sullom Voe

Remne Stacks
Point of Fethaland
Isbister
North Roe
Roer Water
Burra Voe
Housetter
Collafirth
Voe
Ollaberry
A970
Gluss
Sullom
A970
17
M
5
Mangaster
Manaster
Uyea
Ronas Hill
450
Ronas Voe
Roer Water
Eela Water
Urafirth
4
The Father
Heylor
Hamnavoe
Scarff
Burnside
Ure
Braehoulland
Sandvick
Hillswick
Bea Taing
B9078
Brae Wick
Esha Ness
Stenness
Hamna Voe

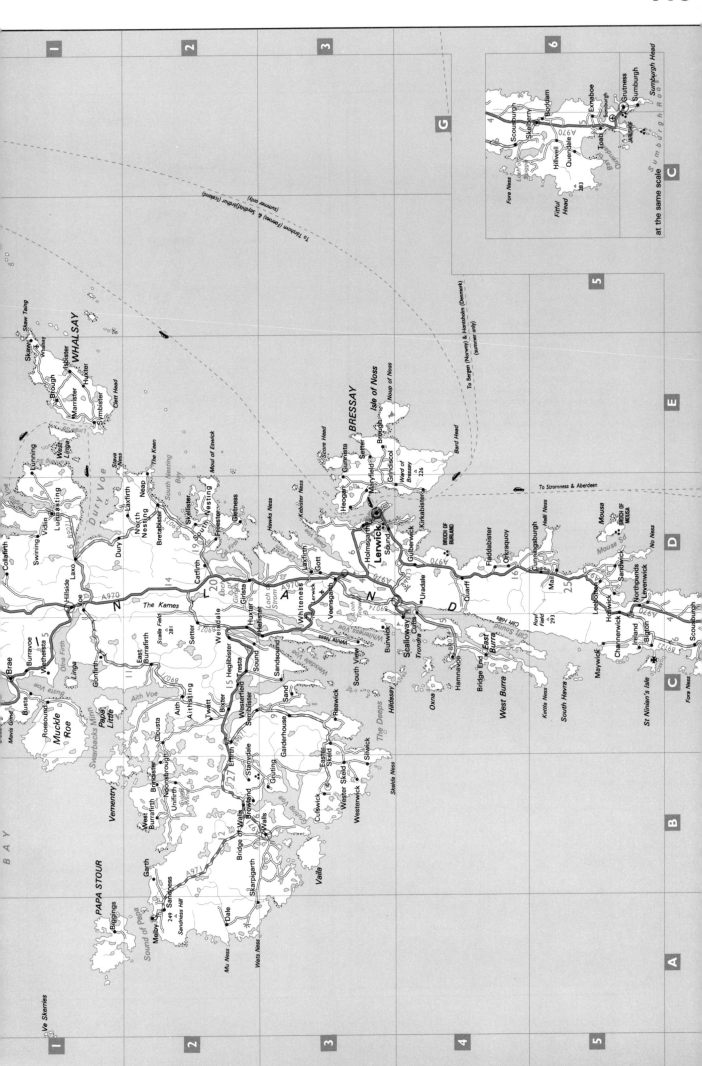

at the same scale

To Tórshavn (Faroes) & Seyðisfjörður (Iceland)
(summer only)

To Bergen (Norway) & Hanstholm (Denmark)
(summer only)

To Stromness & Aberdeen

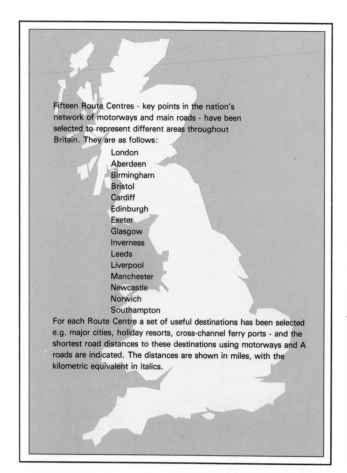

Fifteen Route Centres - key points in the nation's network of motorways and main roads - have been selected to represent different areas throughout Britain. They are as follows:

London
Aberdeen
Birmingham
Bristol
Cardiff
Edinburgh
Exeter
Glasgow
Inverness
Leeds
Liverpool
Manchester
Newcastle
Norwich
Southampton

For each Route Centre a set of useful destinations has been selected e.g. major cities, holiday resorts, cross-channel ferry ports - and the shortest road distances to these destinations using motorways and A roads are indicated. The distances are shown in miles, with the kilometric equivalent in italics.

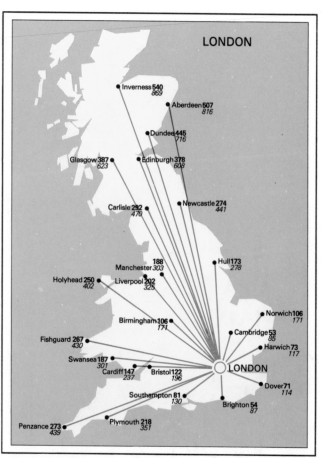

LONDON

Inverness 540 / 869
Aberdeen 507 / 816
Dundee 445 / 716
Glasgow 387 / 623
Edinburgh 378 / 608
Carlisle 292 / 470
Newcastle 274 / 441
Manchester 188 / 303
Hull 173 / 278
Holyhead 250 / 402
Liverpool 202 / 325
Norwich 106 / 171
Birmingham 106 / 171
Cambridge 53 / 85
Fishguard 267 / 430
Harwich 73 / 117
Swansea 187 / 301
Cardiff 147 / 237
Bristol 122 / 196
LONDON
Dover 71 / 114
Southampton 81 / 130
Brighton 54 / 87
Penzance 273 / 439
Plymouth 218 / 351

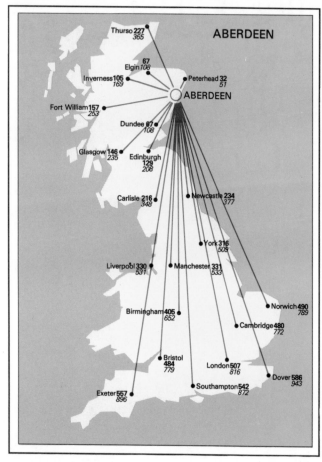

ABERDEEN

Thurso 227 / 365
Elgin 67 / 108
Inverness 105 / 169
Peterhead 32 / 51
Fort William 157 / 253
ABERDEEN
Dundee 67 / 108
Glasgow 146 / 235
Edinburgh 129 / 208
Carlisle 216 / 348
Newcastle 234 / 377
York 316 / 509
Liverpool 330 / 531
Manchester 331 / 533
Norwich 490 / 789
Birmingham 405 / 652
Cambridge 480 / 772
Bristol 484 / 779
London 507 / 816
Dover 586 / 943
Exeter 557 / 896
Southampton 542 / 872

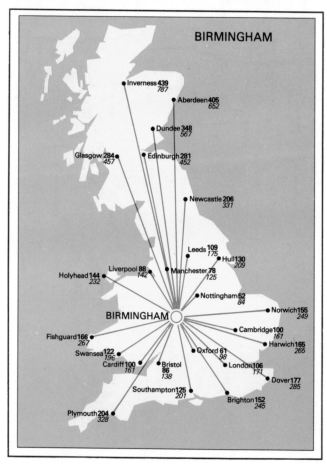

BIRMINGHAM

Inverness 439 / 787
Aberdeen 405 / 652
Dundee 348 / 567
Glasgow 284 / 457
Edinburgh 281 / 452
Newcastle 206 / 331
Leeds 109 / 175
Hull 130 / 209
Holyhead 144 / 232
Liverpool 88 / 142
Manchester 78 / 125
Nottingham 52 / 84
Norwich 155 / 249
BIRMINGHAM
Cambridge 100 / 161
Fishguard 166 / 267
Harwich 165 / 265
Swansea 122 / 196
Oxford 61 / 98
Cardiff 100 / 161
Bristol 86 / 138
London 106 / 171
Dover 177 / 285
Southampton 125 / 201
Brighton 152 / 245
Plymouth 204 / 328

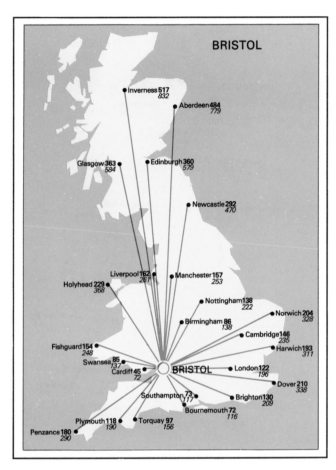

**BRISTOL**

Inverness 517 / 832
Aberdeen 484 / 779
Glasgow 363 / 584
Edinburgh 360 / 579
Newcastle 292 / 470
Liverpool 162 / 261
Manchester 157 / 253
Holyhead 229 / 368
Nottingham 138 / 222
Birmingham 86 / 138
Norwich 204 / 328
Fishguard 154 / 248
Cambridge 146 / 235
Harwich 193 / 311
Swansea 85 / 137
Cardiff 45 / 72
London 122 / 196
**BRISTOL**
Dover 210 / 338
Southampton 73 / 117
Brighton 130 / 209
Bournemouth 72 / 116
Plymouth 118 / 190
Torquay 97 / 156
Penzance 180 / 290

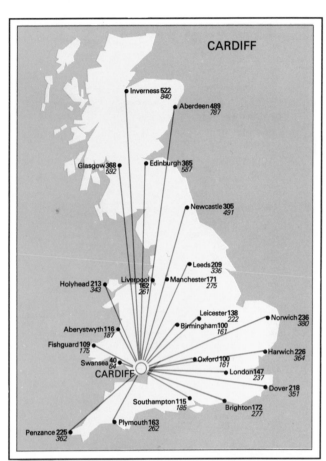

**CARDIFF**

Inverness 522 / 840
Aberdeen 489 / 787
Glasgow 368 / 592
Edinburgh 365 / 587
Newcastle 305 / 491
Leeds 209 / 336
Liverpool 162 / 261
Manchester 171 / 275
Holyhead 213 / 343
Leicester 138 / 222
Norwich 236 / 380
Aberystwyth 116 / 187
Birmingham 100 / 161
Fishguard 109 / 175
Harwich 226 / 364
Swansea 40 / 64
Oxford 100 / 161
London 147 / 237
**CARDIFF**
Dover 218 / 351
Southampton 115 / 185
Brighton 172 / 277
Plymouth 163 / 262
Penzance 225 / 362

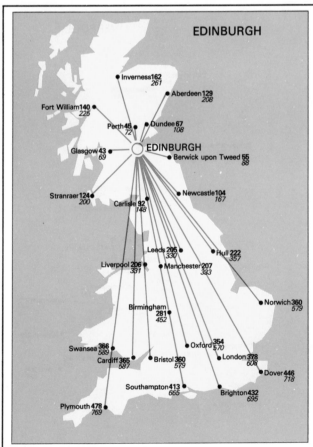

**EDINBURGH**

Inverness 162 / 261
Aberdeen 129 / 208
Fort William 140 / 225
Perth 45 / 72
Dundee 67 / 108
Glasgow 43 / 69
**EDINBURGH**
Berwick upon Tweed 55 / 88
Stranraer 124 / 200
Newcastle 104 / 167
Carlisle 92 / 148
Leeds 205 / 330
Hull 222 / 357
Liverpool 206 / 331
Manchester 207 / 333
Norwich 360 / 579
Birmingham 281 / 452
Swansea 366 / 589
Oxford 354 / 570
Cardiff 365 / 587
Bristol 360 / 579
London 378 / 608
Dover 446 / 718
Southampton 413 / 665
Brighton 432 / 695
Plymouth 478 / 769

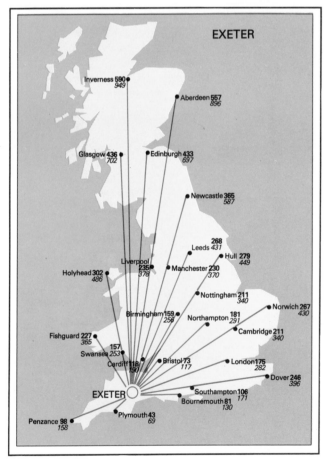

**EXETER**

Inverness 590 / 949
Aberdeen 557 / 896
Glasgow 436 / 702
Edinburgh 433 / 697
Newcastle 365 / 587
Leeds 268 / 431
Hull 279 / 449
Liverpool 235 / 378
Manchester 230 / 370
Holyhead 302 / 486
Nottingham 211 / 340
Birmingham 159 / 256
Northampton 181 / 291
Norwich 267 / 430
Fishguard 227 / 365
Cambridge 211 / 340
Swansea 157 / 253
Cardiff 118 / 190
Bristol 73 / 117
London 175 / 282
Dover 246 / 396
**EXETER**
Southampton 106 / 171
Bournemouth 81 / 130
Penzance 98 / 158
Plymouth 43 / 69

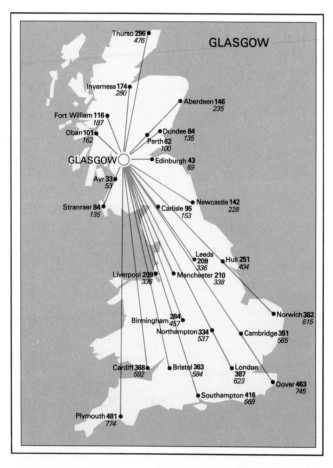

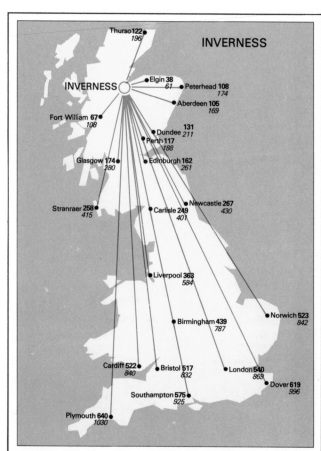

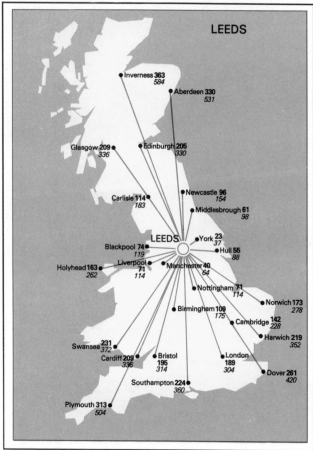

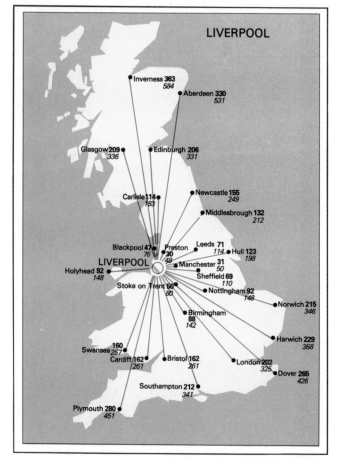

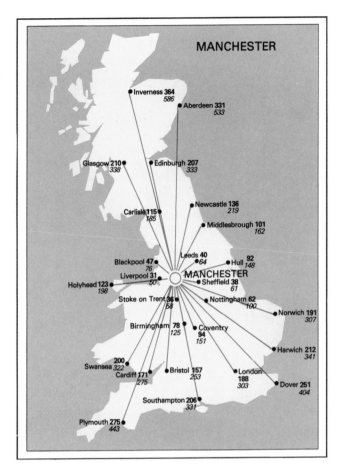

**MANCHESTER**

Inverness **364** *586*
Aberdeen **331** *533*
Glasgow **210** *338*
Edinburgh **207** *333*
Carlisle **115** *185*
Newcastle **136** *219*
Middlesbrough **101** *162*
Blackpool **47** *76*
Leeds **40** *64*
Hull **92** *148*
Liverpool **31** *50*
MANCHESTER
Holyhead **123** *198*
Sheffield **38** *61*
Stoke on Trent **36** *58*
Nottingham **62** *100*
Norwich **191** *307*
Birmingham **78** *125*
Coventry **94** *151*
Harwich **212** *341*
Swansea **200** *322*
Cardiff **171** *275*
Bristol **157** *263*
London **188** *303*
Dover **251** *404*
Southampton **206** *331*
Plymouth **275** *443*

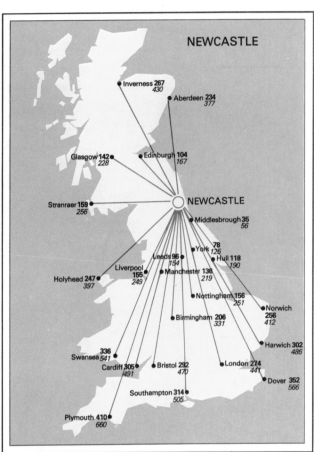

**NEWCASTLE**

Inverness **267** *430*
Aberdeen **234** *377*
Glasgow **142** *228*
Edinburgh **104** *167*
Stranraer **159** *256*
NEWCASTLE
Middlesbrough **35** *56*
York **78** *125*
Leeds **96** *154*
Hull **118** *190*
Liverpool **155** *249*
Manchester **136** *219*
Holyhead **247** *397*
Nottingham **156** *251*
Norwich **256** *412*
Birmingham **206** *331*
Harwich **302** *486*
Swansea **336** *541*
Cardiff **305** *491*
Bristol **292** *470*
London **274** *441*
Southampton **314** *505*
Dover **352** *566*
Plymouth **410** *660*

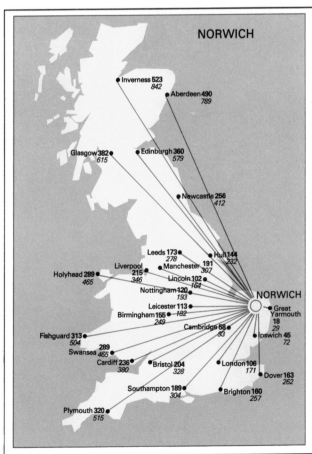

**NORWICH**

Inverness **523** *842*
Aberdeen **490** *789*
Glasgow **382** *615*
Edinburgh **360** *579*
Newcastle **256** *412*
Leeds **173** *278*
Hull **144** *232*
Liverpool **215** *346*
Manchester **191** *307*
Holyhead **289** *465*
Lincoln **102** *164*
Nottingham **120** *193*
Leicester **113** *182*
NORWICH
Great Yarmouth **18** *29*
Birmingham **155** *249*
Cambridge **58** *93*
Ipswich **45** *72*
Fishguard **313** *504*
Swansea **289** *465*
Cardiff **236** *380*
Bristol **204** *328*
London **106** *171*
Dover **163** *262*
Southampton **189** *304*
Brighton **160** *257*
Plymouth **320** *515*

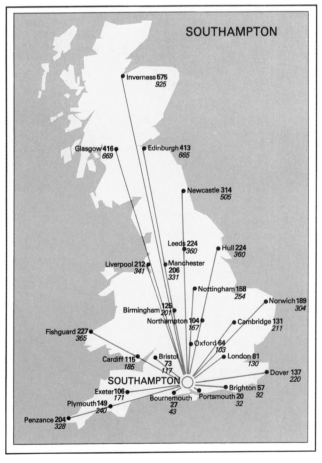

**SOUTHAMPTON**

Inverness **575** *925*
Glasgow **416** *669*
Edinburgh **413** *665*
Newcastle **314** *505*
Leeds **224** *360*
Hull **224** *360*
Liverpool **212** *341*
Manchester **206** *331*
Nottingham **158** *254*
Norwich **189** *304*
Birmingham **125** *201*
Northampton **104** *167*
Cambridge **131** *211*
Fishguard **227** *365*
Oxford **64** *103*
Cardiff **115** *185*
Bristol **73** *117*
London **81** *130*
Dover **137** *220*
SOUTHAMPTON
Exeter **106** *171*
Brighton **57** *92*
Plymouth **149** *240*
Bournemouth **27** *43*
Portsmouth **20** *32*
Penzance **204** *328*

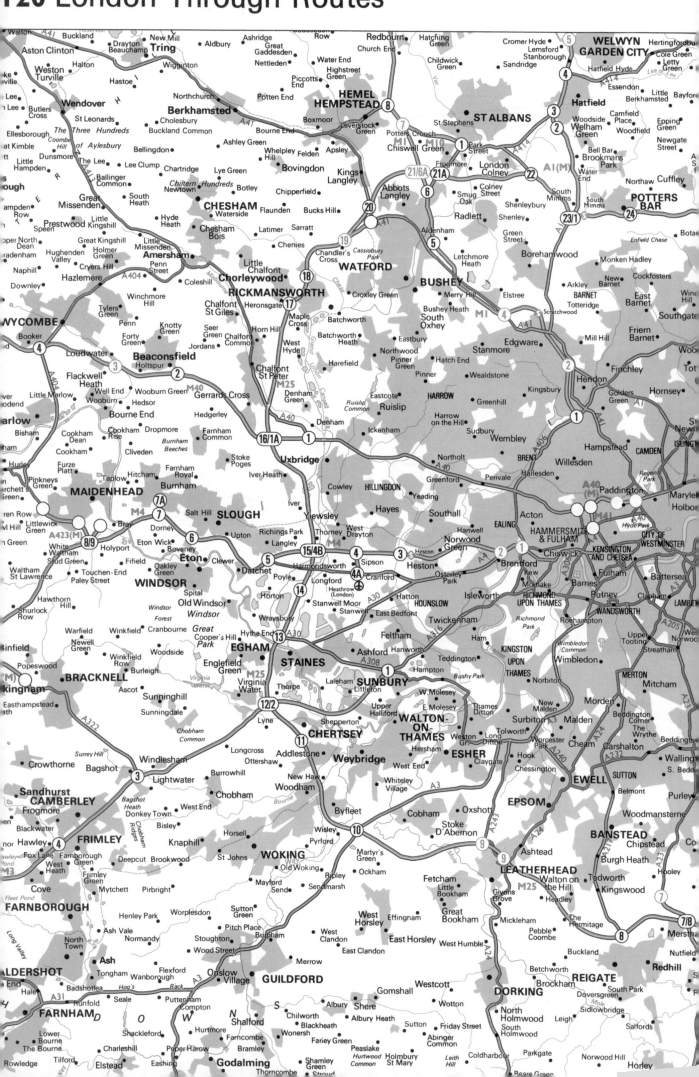

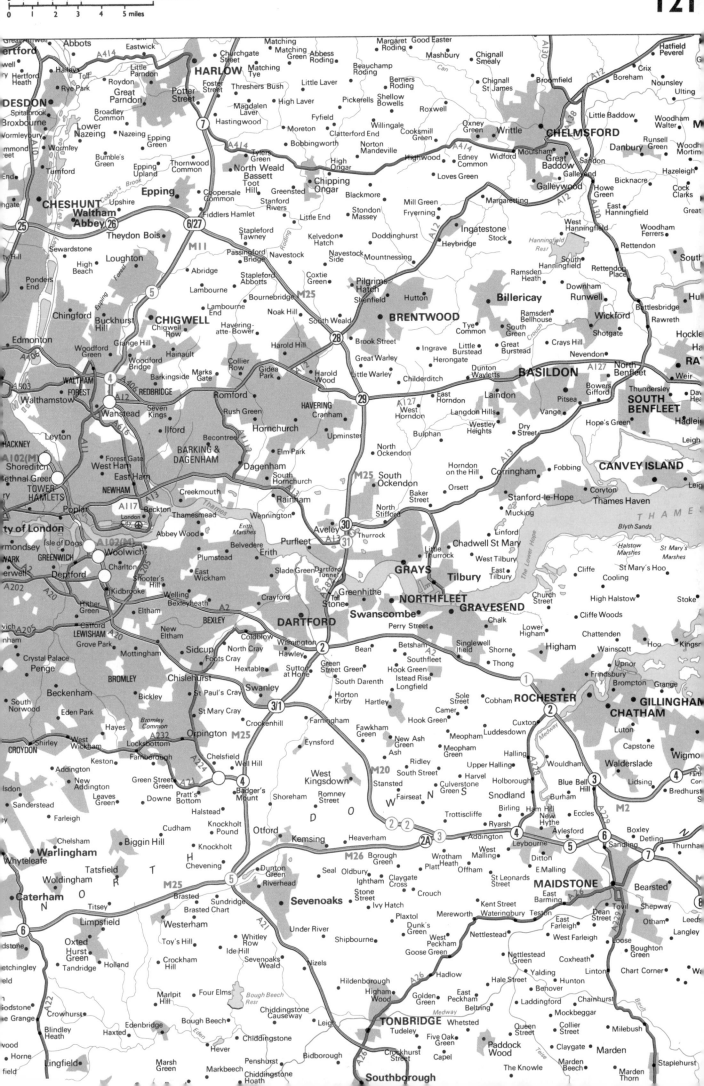

10 kilometres
5 miles

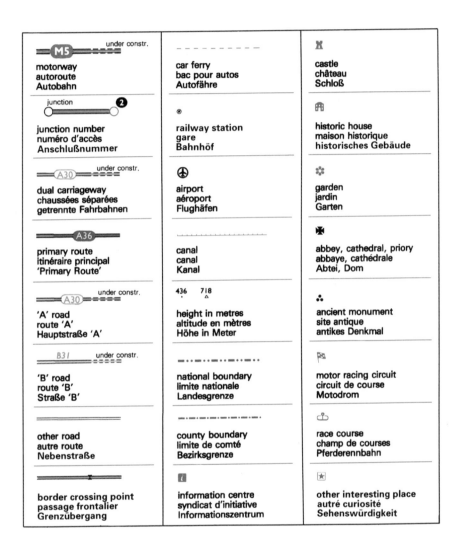

| | | |
|---|---|---|
| **motorway** / autoroute / Autobahn | **car ferry** / bac pour autos / Autofähre | **castle** / château / Schloß |
| **junction number** / numéro d'accès / Anschlußnummer | **railway station** / gare / Bahnhöf | **historic house** / maison historique / historisches Gebäude |
| **dual carriageway** / chaussées séparées / getrennte Fahrbahnen | **airport** / aéroport / Flughäfen | **garden** / jardin / Garten |
| **primary route** / itinéraire principal / 'Primary Route' | **canal** / canal / Kanal | **abbey, cathedral, priory** / abbaye, cathédrale / Abtei, Dom |
| **'A' road** / route 'A' / Hauptstraße 'A' | **height in metres** / altitude en mètres / Höhe in Meter | **ancient monument** / site antique / antikes Denkmal |
| **'B' road** / route 'B' / Straße 'B' | **national boundary** / limite nationale / Landesgrenze | **motor racing circuit** / circuit de course / Motodrom |
| **other road** / autre route / Nebenstraße | **county boundary** / limite de comté / Bezirksgrenze | **race course** / champ de courses / Pferderennbahn |
| **border crossing point** / passage frontalier / Grenzübergang | **information centre** / syndicat d'initiative / Informationszentrum | **other interesting place** / autré curiosité / Sehenswürdigkeit |

9 miles to 1 inch/5.6 km to 1 cm

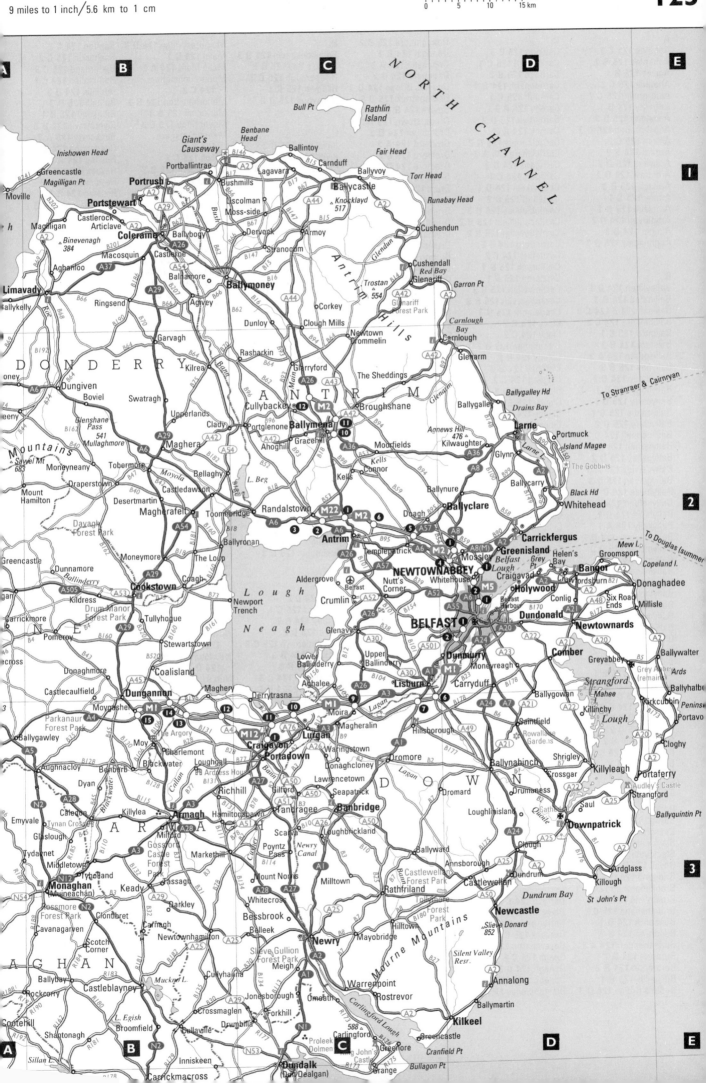

# Northern Ireland Index

# Great Britain Index

# COMPETITION
## ENTRY FORM

To enter, simply fill in the details below and fold as guide [see the reverse of this page] affix stamp and pop the envelope in the post. Winter could be a lot shorter for you as one of our lucky winners enjoying the sunshine in Tenerife. Please Write Your Personal Number [This is on Facing Page to the Inside Front Cover]

Name _____ Mr/Mrs/Ms/Other _____

Address _____

_____

Town _____ County _____ Postcode _____

Make of Car? _____ Model _____ Year _____

Where Did You Purchase The Car? _____

Was it New?  YES ☐    NO ☐    [Please Tick]

Is Your Car?
[A] Privately Owned ☐       [B] Company Owned ☐
[C] Other  [Please Specify] _____

Where Do You Have Your Car Serviced?
[A] Dealer For Your Make of Car. ☐    [B] Dealer For Other Make of Car ☐
[C] Garage Not Selling New Cars ☐    [D] Automotive Superstore/Fast Fit ☐
[E] Mobile Mechanic ☐        [F] DIY ☐
[G] Other [Please Specify] _____

Where Do You Go For More Serious Work?
[A] Dealer For Your Make of Car. ☐    [B] Dealer For Other Make of Car ☐
[C] Garage Not Selling New Cars ☐    [D] Automotive Superstore/Fast Fit ☐
[E] Mobile Mechanic ☐    [F] DIY ☐    [G] Other [Specify] _____

In The Last 6 Months Have You Personally Done Any of the Following?
[A] Changed The Oil ☐  [B] Changed The Air/Oil Filter ☐  [C] Changed The Plugs ☐
[D] Light Bodywork ☐  [E] Changed The Radiator Hose ☐  [F] Changed The Thermostat ☐
[G] Other _____

Where did you obtain this Atlas?    Name _____ Town _____

This information will only be used in accordance with the Data Protection Act.

FOLD 3

FOLD 2

FOLD 1

Affix
Stamp

**Tenerife Competition**
**Promotion Fulfilment**
**Unipart**
**Unipart House**
**Garsington Road**
**Cowley**
**Oxford OX4 2PG**

TUCK IN